ost ge... l

rescuing our children from the grip of darkness

Lost Generation

      Life Building Ministries
      Attention: Jamey Ragle
      PO Box 840, Burlington, KY 41005.
ISBN: 0-9700639-6-2

Cover Design: The Addison Group
               Lee Fredrickson: IBIS Design
Book Design: Ken Amador: IBIS Design

Life Building Ministries
Visit our Web Site:
http://www.jameyragle.org
e-mail us at:
jamey@jameyragle.org

21stCENTURYPRESS.com
P.O. Box 8033
Springfield, MO 65801

Contents

Dedication

This book is dedicated to my wife, Patty.

For over 20 years, she has stood with me through the rigors of life on the road and through the hectic schedule that accompanies my abbreviated times at home. It has not been easy, or without a price. I only hope that I can live long enough to enjoy a season of time when I can give more of myself to make her life as blessed as she has made mine.

To my three daughters, Heather, Heidi, and Holly:

You are my angels! I love you more than words can express. This book is also dedicated to you and for you. I pray that you will end well. Love, Dad.

Acknowledgements

First books are never easy to write.

Upon first consideration, waves of enthusiasm sweep over you. Those buoyant waves are quickly followed by pounding waves of discouragement. There never seems to be enough time in your hectic schedule. On one day, you cannot wait to get your thoughts upon the computer screen, but that day is quickly followed by more days when you cannot imagine whatever made you consider writing a book. As you bob up and down with the emotions of writing a book–first up and then down and then up again–you discover a new depth of appreciation for friends; not just any friends, but the kind of friends who offer you wisdom and constructive criticism, the kind of friends who smack you on the shoulder and encourage you with their smile of, "You can do this!"

Thanks to all of you–you know who you are and you are too numerous to mention–for your financial support, for your suggestions, for your encouragement. Without you, the publication of this book would not have happened.

Jamey Ragle

lost generation

Introduction

Most parents are unaware of the intensity of our nation's cultural problems and the crushing consequences these problems have upon the characters of their children. Most parents are also unaware of the source of our culture's problems, and in their blindness, parents often fraternize and associate with a culture that actually devours the innocence of their children. This parental ignorance actually paralyzes them in the protection of their children from a culture that has lost its moral compass.

No one growing up in the '60s revolution could escape the influence of their changing culture.

Following the '50s, which history records as the decade of searching for material posterity, a plague of immorality swept across America during the Woodstock generation of the '60s. When the youth in this decade rebelled against the establishment and anyone over the age of thirty, they succeeded in tearing down more than America's traditional morals and conventional society. They started a tidal wave that successfully washed away our national conscience. We have

become a nation that can no longer distinguish between good and evil. We now call good evil and evil good.

One decisive factor that intensifies the cultural crisis that we face today is that most parents of today's youth were born during the '60s and '70s. Those were the decades when vast cultural changes occurred in America. Consequently, those growing up during those decades did so in a nation that had moved away from its foundational roots of morality. They could not help but be influenced by the society in which they matured. These baby boomers were continually bombarded with the '60s philosophy as their national heritage. Daily and constantly, their minds were molded through the education, music, entertainment, movies, media and television that embraced and supported the counterculture of the '60s revolution.

None of us is exempt from the influence of the '60s revolution and the profound impact which that decade had upon America.

Those born in the '60s and '70s grew up in a culture that promoted sexual immorality, legal abortions, violence, filthy communication, drugs and immoral music and entertainment. It was a culture that perverted and mocked everything pertaining to traditional Christianity, and its offspring were the unfortunate products of a culture that denied its foundations. Some of the youth of the '60s actively participated in the revolution. More of them simply experienced the cultural changes through the news media, music, movies and television. Some remained within the protective walls of the church. None, however, escaped the influence of their changing culture or the powerful impact of a society rife with upheavals in its traditional morality and system of standards. And not only did they not escape, but ultimately this toppled culture shaped their thinking, their values and their outlook on life.

The changes that occurred during this decade, flowing on into the '70s, were very gradual and pervasive, which is characteristic of how subtly Satan works. With an occasional curse word spoken here and there on television or the progressive immodesty of the fashion industry, for example, Satan brings us along a little bit at a time, and before we realize how deadly the effects of sin are, we are in too deep. Whether we were young people during the '40s, '50s, '70s or '80s, none of us is exempt from the '60s revolution and the profound impact that decade had upon America: The fact we often overlook is that those young people who emerged out of the cultural framework of the '60s are presently the parents of today's youth.

Today's youth are being raised by parents whose values system was greatly impacted by a nation that had suddenly lost its moral and cultural bearings. Baby boomer parents loved their children, yet many unknowingly abdicated their God-given responsibility to train their children. They failed to instill within their children the moral values taught by Christ. Consequently, the youth of today are lost and floundering in a society that offers no hope for their spiritual and moral rescue.

The moral foundation that a nation should provide for its youth is not available for the young people of today. The choices they make in life are rarely based upon the standards upheld in the Word of God, because the American culture and the church in America have departed from our national and moral legacy, which was founded upon the principles written in the Bible. Moreover, this lack of a national moral foundation does not only affect children who do not attend church. Its influence is felt as just as distinctly within the walls of America's churches and Christian schools.

High school girls in one of America's most prominent Christian schools regularly perform oral sex on their boyfriends. They justify their actions because they are not being sexually penetrated by the male organ. Is this philosophy being taught in our churches? Not likely. It comes from the conditioning of a culture that has removed all boundaries from sexual activity. The source of that sexual promiscuity can be found in the '60s, and it has escalated to its present-day crisis. This confirms what I mentioned earlier regarding the subtlety of the Enemy. Now we live in a society in which President Clinton recently used and misused semantics to wriggle his way out of the numerous sexual encounters with Monica Lewinsky. With this kind of leadership, or lack thereof, it is no wonder that the high school girls mentioned above justify what they do.

This book is not being written with condemnation directed toward today's baby boomer parents, regardless of when or where they were born or raised. It is written for the purpose of enlightening parents on why there is such a cultural crisis and informing them as to what they can do to counteract this cultural influence on their children. It is written as a guide for parents on how to salvage their children from a national culture that has lost its conscience. It is written to try to make some sense out of a senseless society and to try to recover the fragile destinies of our young people.

The words of a song recorded by a well known secular artist partly convey the idea of this book:

> If I live in a time and place
> Where you don't want to be
> You don't have to walk along this road with me
> My yesterday won't have to be your way
> If I knew–
> I'd have tried to change the world I brought you to
> And there isn't very much that I can do
> But I would– if I could[1]

The youth of today did not choose to be born into the cultural time and place that the past three decades have established for them. As a parent, I say that our "yesterday won't have to be their way." We can change the world into which we brought our children. We must change it for their sakes and for their childrens' sakes. The song also says sadly, "But I would–if I could." The proposal of this book is "But we can and we must" change the world for our children. Just as surely as our forefathers paid the price to change a nation for us, we can change it for our children and our children's children. Even as our forefathers determined to become the defining link that connected the origins of this nation to its future for our sakes, we must become a link for our children. We must reach back to the past and the heritage of our national, moral foundations and become that bridge from the past to a stable, blessed future for the sake of our children.

PART I
PANORAMA
OF THE PROBLEM

Chapter One

Revolution of our Culture

Our founding forefathers were not obligated to give us a secure future. They obligated themselves only to give us a secure foundation upon which to build a nation. And having done so, they relinquished the future responsibility of guarding this nation to us, the generations who would follow them. The majority of our forefathers were Christians who realized the necessity of establishing a nation upon the principles provided in the Word of God. They cautiously studied all forms of government and prayerfully pondered the strengths and weaknesses of each. History records that they interrupted their constitutional sessions with fasting and prayer to seek God's direction and wisdom. Regardless of whether or not we realize it, or whether or not the media acknowledge it, our forefathers determined that America would be birthed as a

Christian nation, as "one nation under God," *not* "one nation without conscience" as it is today. Our nation was birthed in a contractual agreement with God that we were to be a Christian nation with laws and principles founded upon the Judaeo-Christian faith.

One of the enduring keys to the sacrificial patriotism of our forefathers was that they understood the importance of being a bridge that connected the past to the future. They were well aware of the fact that they were carving out a nation for the generations who would follow, and they looked upon it as their duty to prepare for the future generations. They had immigrated from countries that had religious intolerance, and they were determined to have religious freedom for their children. Their speeches, their diaries and their private letters record the truth: they realized the importance of being a link in the chain that connects the past to the future.

Our nation's founding forefathers understood that God is a God of the generations.

Our forefathers also understood that God is a God of generations. Often in the scriptures, God refers to Himself as the "God of Abraham, Isaac, and Jacob." There was a purposeful connection between God and those three generations. His plan and purposes always include more than one individual; they encompass generations. An old Chinese proverb also tells of this truth: "One generation plants the trees and the next generation enjoys the shade." Our forefathers planted the tree for us as a nation, and for almost two hundred years, we have enjoyed the shade of those moral standards. Now it is time for us to plant trees of moral restoration for our children's' children and grandchildren. Our forefathers understood their duty to future generations. We can do no less.

One of the byproducts of the baby boomer phenomena is that individuals became obsessed with the present and lived only for the moment. They became characterized by a search for instant gratification, and this gave rise to the prominent attitude expressed by a prominent fast food chain some years ago: "You deserve a break today." And the real cultural message conveyed by this little slogan was, "You deserve to acquire all the 'goodies' without paying any price." My experience over the years, especially in observing dating relationships, is that gratification and this type of mentality always lead to immorality. The sad truth is that young men and women of today are delving into physical relationships without thoroughly understanding the consequences of their behavior. The gratification may be instant, but the consequences can be deadly.

The young people in the '60s rejected the past. They rejected everything that their parents and America symbolized to them. Worse still, they not only rejected what their parents stood for, but the breakdown of the family began when they even rejected their parents themselves. They walked out of their parents' homes by the scores and began living in communes together. Rebellion against anyone over thirty became the mind-set of the youth growing up in the '60s. Their own desires blinded them to the sacrifices that had been made by their ancestors. They showed no regard for the sacrifices that their parents and forefathers paid to purchase and maintain the freedom to make their public and private protests. And when the youth of the '60s rejected the past, they also rejected their responsibility for building a future. Because they lived only for the moment, they gave no thought to the consequences of being a generation cut off from its past and irresponsible regarding its future.

The youth of the '60s had a definitive goal. It was to tear down everything that their parents had built. They said "no" to everything their parents had said "yes" to. They criticized the old social order and screamed for a new one, yet it never occurred to them that they had no blueprint for their utopian dream to usher in the "age of Aquarius":

> When the moon is in the seventh house,
> And Jupiter aligns with Mars,
> Then peace will guide the planets
> And love will steer the stars;
> This is the dawning of the age of Aquarius,
> Harmony and understanding, sympathy and
> trust abounding.[1]

They dreamed of and wrote the songs of a new social order, but their immaturity failed to supply them with the moral absolutes that were necessary to found that new social order. The lyrics of their songs pleaded with humankind to reach for a higher order, yet their rejection of anything in their parents' past denied them the boundaries that had been wisely laid by our forefathers.

No one can deny that there were many good beliefs embraced by the idealistic youth of the '60s who yearned for "harmony and understanding, sympathy and trust abounding." They protested for the civil rights of others. They helped to register black voters in the South.

They served in the Peace Corps. Deep within, they wanted to do something good for others. Many sincerely turned their hearts toward the goal of changing society, and they demonstrated to the world how young people can change a nation.

So what went wrong? Had the materialism of their parents been wrong after all? Were these young men and women not right to reject a society that they viewed as being too materialistic? The problem lies in the fact that rather than being selective, these youth said "no" to *everything* that their parents had embraced. In doing so, they ultimately said "no" to the absolute truths founded in the Bible. They made the fatal mistake of cutting themselves off from their national heritage.

When something in nature swings too far to the right, then it ultimately swings too far back toward the left. Youth turned their backs on the materialism that had become the focus of their parents.

I remember, as a young person, that the friendliest kids in high school seemed to be those who lived lives completely contrary to what I had been taught as a child growing up in church. I remember how the athletes, or the "jocks" as we called them, and the rich prep students were never as friendly as the "druggies" or the "freaks" in school. Experience has taught me that many young men and women associate with and hang out with these "freaks" or "hippies" as we called them, not because they agree with their actions but because the misfits tend to readily accept others

on a personal level. No social or financial status is required to become a part of this group; they mean it when they say, "Come as you are."

Let us look backward, ourselves, so that we as parents might have a better understanding of how our culture has degenerated to its current state of crisis and of the framework in which it now influences our children.

The Fifties

World War II had ended. America had elected one of her war heroes, General Dwight D. Eisenhower, to the oval office, and the Eisenhower era ushered in national peace and unprecedented prosperity. The return of America's soldiers to the arms of their sweethearts and wives also ushered in the conception of the children who would later become known as the baby boomers. Those who were parents in the '50s had endured an incomparable world war. Some had paid a high price to protect the freedom that Americans so cherished, and they were ready for some peace and quiet.

After the Great Depression and World War II, parents wanted something better for their children. Most parents gave their children what they had been deprived of in their youth, the accumulation of material goods and wealth, and they believed this made them good parents. In almost every household across America, parents told their children, "I want you to have more than I had when I was growing up." That utterance silently stamped parents' consciences with the "Good Parent" seal of approval. From the parents' viewpoint, they were sacrificing in order to give to their children. When these baby boomer children grew up, however, they accused their parents of substituting materialism for love.

When something in nature swings too far to the right, then it ultimately swings too far back toward the left, and this pendulum effect began to take place in American homes during the '60s. Youth growing up in the late '50s and early '60s turned their backs on the materialism that had become the focus of their parents' attention. Feeling misunderstood, they were determined to see change. Since the White House, Congress and the Pentagon were beyond their grasp, they turned their attention toward the family. They could start their revolution to change society by rejecting their own personal families who represented all that they opposed. One of the activists during the '60s, Annie Gotlieb, wrote about their agenda to disrupt the family structure:

> If the right wing gets to write history, they will put us down, not as the 'Love Generation,' but as the generation that destroyed the American family. They will point to the soaring rates of divorce, venereal disease, teen pregnancy, and abortion as sequelae [sic] of the Sixties. If they are right in their attribution of blame, then, ironically, the Sixties generation achieved one of its main objectives.

> We might not have been able to tear down the state, but the family was closer. We could get our hands on it....We truly believed that the family had to be torn apart to free love, which alone could heal the damage done when the atom was split to release energy.[2]

Naturally, Hollywood picked up on the discontentment of young people and began producing movies that depicted the growing gap between teens and their parents. James

Dean became immortalized as a teenage idol because of his role in "Rebel Without A Cause." Movies such as "Summer's Place" emphasized the double standards that parents held for themselves and their children. These and other productions helped to spread aggressive rebellion among young people.

The Sixties

Life in America suddenly and forever changed on November 22, 1963, when gunshots shattered the air in Dallas, Texas. The Prince of Camelot had been assassinated. Many have documented the death of John F. Kennedy as the death of America's innocence. The time of passive resistance came to an abrupt end. By the middle of the decade, protests against the Vietnam War and race riots erupted throughout the country. Many were killed. Injuries due to the race riots and the war protests soared upward into the thousands. Then the assassinations of Martin Luther King and Robert Kennedy in 1968 further escalated the bitterness of America's youth. On college campuses throughout the country, professors incited more unrest by preaching their own doctrine regarding the Vietnam War, and students were urged to align themselves with the plight of the North Vietnamese. Students driven by this paranoia found relief in casting their lots with the political left, and the marriage

As the decade of the '60s drew to a close, the youth had solidified their allegiance to their new way of thinking. Living together became a way of life for young people.

between the flower children and the political left produced a new counterculture.

In addition to the marriage between the flower children and the political left, the music of the '60s quickly became the opiate to soothe the youth's troubled souls. Songs about the injustice and inequity of the establishment were produced by the hundreds. Lyrics coming over the airwaves had a hypnotic effect on those who cried out for justice and equality. Folk singers strummed their guitars and preached their sermons through their songs:

> If I had a hammer...
> I'd hammer out a warning....
> It's the hammer of justice,
> It's the bell of freedom...[3]
> How many deaths will it take till he knows
> That too many people have died?[4]

As the youth of the '60s solidified their allegiance to their new way of thinking, living together became a way of life for young people. Sexual freedom was openly flaunted before parents and the public. The '60s had successfully negated moral restraints on sexuality and destroyed all the forefathers' landmarks. Nervous parents politely apologized and then gradually accepted this bizarre behavior. Homosexuality, drugs, sex, music, long hair and blue jeans became the identifying marks of young people. As the '60s drew to a close, however, the noble dream of changing society for the good began to evaporate. Musicians ended up dead from overdoses of drugs, and many college students ended up as promiscuous derelicts or pathetic alcoholics. The focus gradually shifted from the philosophy of helping others

23

to a very new one held by a culture that was absorbed in self. It was a decade that opened with idealistic youth chanting for change in society, but it ended in drug dependency and disillusionment.

The sweet psalmist of Israel, King David, penned the words: "When the foundations are being destroyed, what can the righteous do?"[5] When nine and eleven-year-old boys shoot and kill their classmates, we must admit that our foundations have surely crumbled. When teenaged mothers give birth to babies and toss them into garbage pails, we must admit that our foundations have definitely collapsed. There can be little doubt that America's moral foundations have been destroyed. And they began disintegrating during the '60s revolution.

The Seventies

With sexuality now openly permitted, the national conscience had to be soothed. Books began filling the shelves with such titles as *I'm Okay, You're Okay* and *Your Inner Child*. The era was characterized by a sudden, insatiable desire to justify and love the self. It was considered okay to have sex outside the boundaries of marriage—books promoted it; movies promoted it; television promoted it. Youth had dropped out of service for others and into savoring the self. Legalized abortion granted woman the choice to control not only her body but also the life of an innocent baby within her. This became a part of a woman's right to "love" herself, and society taught her that she was the god of her own body.

As the youth of the '60s matured, they also began to look within to fill the spiritual vacuum they had helped to create. Because the institution of the Church had

24

been a part of "the establishment," they looked everywhere but inside traditional Christianity, and the New Age movement became the answer. To fill this spiritual vacuum, they began proclaiming that man is god. Spiritual organizations and cults sprang up by the scores. Eastern mysticism met and married with western Christianity, and the marriage was generally a perversion. Jesus was declared not to be God, and man became his own god. One of the most nationally acclaimed incidents of perverted religion was the Jim Jones affair that ended in Jonestown when nearly nine hundred people drank poisoned Kool-Aid in an expression of their dedication.

Spiritualism of every flavor was dished out to the American people. A spiritual vacuum had been created by the '60s revolution, and it was filled up with transcendental meditation, holistic health, Satanism, psychics, channeling, astrology and many other metaphysical teachings. These journeys into eastern mysticism and the occult left people fearful to judge anyone regarding spiritual predilection. A silent code of accepting anyone's spiritual preference crept into our society under the guise that it is unpatriotic to do otherwise. After all, freedom of religion was written into the Constitution of our country.

The legacy of the '70s to young people was that the pinnacle of selfishness is okay. After all, "man is his own god." This was the decade that taught the baby boomers to "love yourself first." Healing was to be found in becoming self-absorbed so that one might heal the inner child. The idea was to focus on the god within and remember, "I'm okay; you're okay." The '70s has been written down by historians as the "me" generation. And it worked. Now our society is filled with citizens who believe they must "look out for number one" and question, "If I don"t take care of me, who will?"

The Eighties

Baby boomers, who are parents of today's youth, are also the ones who watched television, who frequented the movies, who conversed with their friends, who learned their world view in the classrooms and who listened to the music all under the cultural umbrella of the '60s. For the most part, these baby boomers taught their world view to their children, who are, again, the youth of today. Many of today's parents, even Christian parents, do not know how to pass on a moral legacy because they are the children of a society that chose immorality. They were part of a generation that was disconnected with a past that had emphasized morality in the home and therefore in society.

As a child, when I got into trouble at school, I also got into trouble at home. Today's young people may get into trouble at school, but the bad guy is not the child; it is the teacher. It is the person who represents authority. Again, these are the byproducts of our society's kind of thinking. Also, I am still surprised at the number of parents who allow their children to go without supervision, not knowing where they are or setting boundaries or guidelines as to where they can go or how long they can stay gone. And parents do not enforce the rules when they are broken. We have always had a policy at our house: Our girls do not spend the night in the homes of friends whose parents are not saved. We will not knowingly permit this. We do not want our children to be exposed to influences in someone's home that we would not permit in our own home. This may sound old-fashioned, but I determined a long time ago that I may not always be my child's friend, but I will always be her parent. Sometimes, in an effort to lead our children, we have to relinquish what we may view as friendship for their betterment later on.

Unlike this system of discipline and order which we should pursue, the '80s were filled with moral chaos. The boundaries were down; there were no moral absolutes to restrict a culture gone wild. Hollywood continued in its production of nothing but violence, sex, and filthy language, and then sold the world the lie that it was "art" while parents blissfully assumed that they were the major influence in the lives of their children. Along with pushing its perverted art on America, Hollywood openly mocked Christianity and derided those who claimed to be "born-again." Music became a cesspool for kids with destitute souls who dressed like demons from Hell and who screamed out vile lyrics of hate and sexual perversion. Having bowel movements on the stage and throwing it into the audience became acceptable behavior. These musicians became the role models for young children. Along with musicians, professional athletes shared the role model pedestal. Many of them became saturated with a pro-drug attitude. Movie and television stars stripped

Parents of young people today do not give their children a moral legacy because they have become disconnected with a past that taught morals to children in the home.

off their clothes and had shameless sex in front of thousands. And America's children spent many, many more hours with these individuals than with their parents. Finally, the '80s closed with the blood of millions of unborn, aborted children in American.

The Nineties

By the '90s, the idea of moral instruction by parents had nearly become a lost art. The only world view offered to young people of the 90's was a culture that promoted sexuality, disrespect, spiritualism, selfishness and greed. As a nation, we have taught our children that there is no such thing as right and wrong.

It gets worse. CNN recently reported the marked increase of parents who murder their young children. The opposite side of the coin is that young children now take shotguns and knives and brutally murder their parents. Some of those same children then travel on to school and open fire on their fellow students. Schools have become asylums of fear as students walk the hallways. They experience real fear that they could be killed by one of their fellow classmates. And this violence does not just occur in public schools. I know of a student in a Christian school who locked herself in a classroom and committed suicide. Another teen, a 13-year-old boy, who professed to know the Lord as his Savior and outwardly manifested a zeal and thirst for things of the Lord, sexually molested a five-year-old girl.

What consequences have followed the '60s revolution? Where do we stand in the new millennium as a nation? By looking back, we see the unavoidable truth about ourselves as a nation. Our national conscience has been destroyed. Rebellion permeated our culture during the '60s, and its aftermath is still being felt today. We have become a profane society. Disrespect for authority reigns throughout the country. Unrestrained sexuality opened the door to an epidemic of sexually transmitted diseases. Pornography has become a billion-dollar industry. A widespread breakdown of most inhibitions against adultery has occurred within our country. There is a common acceptance in our society of all forms of sexual perversion. Homosexuality is justified, accepted and vigorously promoted. Easy, "causeless" divorce is prevalent. False religion and pseudo-spirituality have saturated our culture. There have been alarming increases among juvenile delinquents. Teenage pregnancy has spiraled upwards and is out of control. The entertainment we view in our movie theaters has long since exceeded the bloody violence of the Roman amphitheaters. And today's music for young people contains filthy, obscene lyrics. Songs for our young people promote violence, rebellion, and perverted sex.

The murders that occurred within the womb for the past twenty years are now occurring outside the womb in view of everyone.

This is the culture in which we raise our children. The apostle Paul wrote about us almost two thousand years ago:

> This know also, that in the last days perilous times shall come. For men shall be lovers of their own selves, covetous, boasters, proud, blasphemers, disobedient to

29

> parents, unthankful, unholy, without natural affection, truce breakers, false accusers, incontinent, fierce, despisers of those that are good, traitors, heady, highminded, lovers of pleasures more than lovers of God; having a form of godliness, but denying the power thereof... [6]

Everything in our society today has been labeled a "syndrome" rather than sin. The implication is that we are all victims, and we are not responsible for what we do. That's why rioting gang members in Los Angeles can almost beat to death a truck driver and be released on all but the most minor charges because the judge said that they were caught up in the mayhem of the moment and were not responsible for their actions. A physician friend of mine recently told me that there are legitimate cases of Attention Deficit and Hyperactivity Disorder in children that require prescription intervention, but he also said that for every legitimate case there are 100 parents who would rather drug their children than to make them behave. I would have to say, looking back over the past few decades, that the idea of "syndrome" is actually right, but the spelling is wrong: our problem is "sindrome." And while we are in many ways victims, we are still responsible for our actions and for the proper raising of our children.

IN SUMMARY

> Our forefathers established our country on the Judaeo-Christian principles found in the Word of God. They understood the secret of being a bridge that connected the past to the future.

Baby boomers rejected the past and lived only for the moment. In doing so, they also rejected the responsibility for building a secure future for their children and their grandchildren.

The definitive goal of youth during the '60s revolution was to tear down everything their parents stood for and to destroy the old social order. They screamed for a new social order, but they offered no plan for anything except what they wanted in that moment.

Because the children of the '60s revolution could not tear down the White House and other government institutions, they turned their attention to destroying the family unit as it had been known by their parents.

The cultural revolution of our century was birthed during the '60s. When the disillusioned youth of the '60s did not succeed in establishing their noble dream of changing society, they turned to savoring the self, and the "me" generation of the '70s was born.

During the '70s, mysticism and the New Age movement filled the spiritual vacuum created by the '60s revolution.

The '80s and '90s were filled with the devastating chaos of a nation that had unraveled its moral fabric.

Chapter Two

Rationalization of our Conscience

The conscience was created within our spirits for the purpose of performing an important task. It corrects and reprimands so as to cause us to feel uneasy when we do something that falls short of the glory of God or when we transgress His moral laws and commandments. The conscience is not the voice of God within us, however. It is the mechanism that allows us to either tune His voice in or tune it out. It provides the inner sensitivity to the spiritual realities of God. When we consider taking an action or committing an error, it is the conscience that immediately protests from deep within our spirit. We become uneasy at any thought or inclination to do wrong. This is God's built-in monitor, and it helps us stay within the boundaries of His holiness. It is in the conscience that God expresses His holiness. Again, the God-given primary function of the

conscience enables us to distinguish between good and evil and incline toward good.

While we were unregenerate sinners our spirits were dead to things of the Lord, yet we know that all persons are influenced by their consciences. We conclude, therefore, that while the conscience cannot function optimally within a spirit that is dead, it does function within the lost sinner in a sluggish, somewhat coma-like way. It maintains its movement within the dead spirit, but not to its fullest capacity. The key, though, to the operation of the conscience, is knowledge.

Knowledge of Good and Evil

The conscience is the mechanism created by God that causes us to consider an action or to refrain from committing an error.

While the conscience is the organ for distinguishing between good and evil, this distinction is determined by what knowledge the conscience has received. The degree of the knowledge of the conscience determines the conviction of the conscience. For example, let us consider a culture in which men take multiple wives. The conscience of a man in that society would not be not troubled at all if he married several women. The cultural knowledge of his society that more than one wife is permissible would silence the inward monitor of the conscience. On the other hand, in America a man would, hopefully, feel reproved for being guilty of bigamy if he had more than one wife. Why would the conscience of this man from a polygamous culture not feel condemned for having numerous wives? The answer is that he would remain comfortable because the conscience condemns us only to the extent of its knowledge. It cannot condemn something that it has never become conscious of, such as polygamy.

Nations and cultures, like individuals, also develop consciences. In the example of the man who lives in a polygamous culture, the national conscience of his country supports the idea that he can have more than one wife. As individuals, our standard of conduct usually rises in accordance with the degree of knowledge of the Scriptures and God's commandments which we possess, and a national conscience is usually composed of a sort of majority conscience. One's knowledge of the Scripture will determine how stable he is, both mentally and socially. Psalm 1 says, "Blessed is the man that walketh not in the counsel of the ungodly." And the chapter goes on to assert that the man who does not walk in the counsel of the ungodly is like a planted tree, which implies stability. The ungodly do not have the benefit of godly knowledge, lacking the presence of the Holy Spirit and admonition of other believers, but they are like the chaff which the wind drives away. And even believers who are not in tune with God's plan for their lives through the reading of His Word will be marked by a lack of stability and permanency. The idea here is that a nation, as moved by its individuals, will operate in accordance with the level of enlightenment of its conscience.

Consider the knowledge that is being supplied for the consciences of America's young people. They have knowledge that pre-martial sex is okay. They have knowledge that sexual immorality is approved. They have become more knowledgeable about violence through entertainment and the news media than any prior generation. If our culture acknowledges such behavior as being acceptable, then it ultimately dulls the consciences of our young people and therefore the sense of obligation to behave otherwise.

Our founding fathers built this nation upon the premise that America would be guided by a Christian conscience. They gave great freedom to us. However, they recognized and spoke among themselves about the fact that the freedom they were bequeathing to future generations could last only under the restraint of a people who had a morally strong conscience.

What has happened to our national conscience? It has become hardened through three decades of Hollywood's standards and the media forcing its own hardened and immoral conscience upon us. When unrestrained sexuality, immoral behavior and intense violence are paraded in front of young children from the time they are born as being the standard of performance. Then, of course, they accept all this knowledge about the moral standards as being their standard. Our children's consciences have become seared and hardened because of the culture that has conditioned their consciences to acknowledge such behavior.

As a nation, we have moved beyond knowing the difference between good and evil. We have rationalized our national conscience into a coma. As a nation we accept evil as good and discredit good as evil. Our national conscience can no longer function in its God-given capacity. We witness teenagers on national television who scream and curse at their parents while teenagers on another program openly brag about the vivid details of their sexual escapades with numerous partners. Boasting about fornication, adultery and extra-marital affairs is done continually on national television. Furthermore, audiences applaud such actions as being brave and standing up to old-fashioned morals. What used to be a sin is now considered ingenious. Lies and deceptions have been woven into the fabric of our everyday lives and labeled "cunning." It is considered smart to cheat the government on one's taxes. Adultery is macho, and 9- and 10-year-old boys can murder an 11-year-old girl simply because they want her bicycle. Our children grow up in a nation that has lost its conscience.

The Bible tells us that, as individuals, we can become hardened by the deceitfulness of sin, and this principle is applicable on a broader social plane. Consequently, our nation has been hardened over the past three decades due to the deceitfulness of our cultural sins. Sin has defiled and hardened our national conscience, and we have therefore become even more susceptible to every kind of sin of pride, greed, and sexual immorality. The greatest aspect of this tragedy is that our children suffer because of our national hardness to sin. Our children have been taught no standards of morality. Their consciences are barely given the opportunity to be awakened, guided and taught except that the light is snuffed out by our cultural sins.

Finally, the moral descent of our nation actually feeds upon itself. Our national conscience hardened in response to the dynamics that were set in operation with the '60s revolution. Now that we have spent three decades hardening our conscience as a nation, we are even more susceptible to accepting all the evil that Hell can rally its forces to launch against us. As the voices of morality are snuffed out by the clamor of our culture's standards, our children cannot hope to mature as shining examples of moral purity, integrity and selflessness. They cannot help but be impacted by a culture with no conscience.

IN SUMMARY

The conscience is the mechanism created by God that causes us to consider an action or to refrain from committing an error. It is God's built-in monitor to keep us within the boundaries of His holiness.

Our conscience is the organ for distinguishing between good and evil, but our conscience convicts us based upon its knowledge. Its knowledge is what will predicate how it acts upon us.

Nations and cultures develop a conscience just like individuals.

Our forefathers established America upon the proposition that our citizens would be guided by their Christian consciences.

As a nation, our conscience has become so seared that we believe evil is good and good is evil.

The consequence of our hardened national conscience is that our children suffer in a dearth of moral standards in the land.

Chapter Three

The Redemption of our Culture

Redeeming a culture covered in darkness is a colossal task, and there are two schools of thought regarding this issue. Many Christians believe that we are to "come out from among them," so they choose to have nothing to do with the world, its system, its government or its culture. They are content to stay within the protective walls of their churches. A second camp maintains that the Lord placed us in this world to be ambassadors for Him. Jesus told his disciples to go out into the world and be salt and light in a dark world that was corrupted with evil:

> Ye are the salt of the earth: but if the salt have lost its savour, wherewith shall it be salted? It is

therefore good for nothing, but to be cast out, and to be trodden under foot of men. Ye are the light of the world. A city that is set on an hill cannot be hid. Neither do men light a candle, and put it under a bushel, but on a candlestick; and it giveth light unto all that are in the house. Let your light so shine before men, that they may see your good works, and glorify your Father which is in heaven.[1]

This second camp interprets the words of Christ to instruct believers to go into the world to counteract the corruption therein. They support the idea that those who follow the Lord and claim to be His disciples should characterize the exact opposite of what our culture promotes. Our values system and lifestyle should be distinctly different from the corrupted one of our culture. We should live our lives and teach our children by a different ethic and a pure morality rather than the system the world has adopted.

A careful reading of the Sermon on the Mount proves that Jesus held up a different standard for His disciples than the standard of the world. That standard was not limited to the disciples; it is to be the Christian's standard, as well. In the sermon, Jesus laid out the standard for our ethical behavior, our religious devotion, our civil responsibility toward others, our attitude toward money and our relationships with one another. Jesus taught us to be distinctly set apart from the world as His disciples. He knew that living under the divine rule of the Lord would itself produce a counterculture to today's culture. Knowing this, we children of God must ask ourselves, "Am I doing this? Do my family and I practice the standards presented in this sermon? Or is it just a passage in our Bible?"

Unfortunately, the church is immersed in the cesspool of our culture. And lest we point our fingers at the corporate church and try to pass the buck, let us also recognize of what, or whom, the church is comprised. We profess to be disciples of the Lord Jesus Christ, yet we are not proactive within our culture. And the simple reason for this is that we, as individuals, have embraced the same set of values as our culture. There is little distinction between the home lives of church members and those of unbelievers. Our families are falling apart. Our children are raised with television's standards of morality like the children of nonbelievers, as we watch the same television programs and attend the same "R" rated movies. Our outlook and world view reflect that of our modern culture more clearly than that of our heavenly heritage.

With regard to evangelism, a gradual shifting in the direction of the world has taken place within the church and amongst evangelicals. Many have made accommodation an inherent part of evangelism. In order to evangelize better, they have adopted some of the world's standards, and in doing this, they have become more susceptible to the culture's influence on them rather than influencing the culture toward righteousness. In this accommodation, the church has adopted a Christianized version of secular culture, and the Christian way of life has become a subculture rather than a counterculture.

This weakness in the modern church is evidenced in the fact that, quite often, the world comes up with ideas which are adopted by Christendom a short time later. For example, talk shows on television were started by

41

the world, so Christian television has adopted this same format, dressing it in Christian garments and language. I do not make this observation merely to condemn but to point out that we Christians are following the world rather than leading it.

As Christians, we have looked into the face of our culture and become its mirror image. We reflect the opinions of the world with regard to what is good and what is evil. We reflect the same standards as the world with regard to our entertainment, our clothing, our music, our lifestyles and our morality. Smoking marijuana is accepted by our Christian young people, and drinking alcohol is approved by those who sit on the church pews.

Our culture's standards of casual and heavy "petting" have also been accepted by our youth. To get a demonstration of this, we only need to try speaking to today's youth about Jacob's love that motivated him to wait seven years for Rachel. Most would stare at us in perplexity. If we were to ask any young boy if he could tell the difference between two girls, one whom he had kissed and "petted" with and the other with whom he had not, he would begin to understand how it was that Jacob did not realize he was with Leah, instead of Rachel, on the first night of his honeymoon. Jacob could not tell which girl was with him in the dark because he had never been intimate with either. Never having "petted" with Rachel, he could not tell her from Leah. Jacob had never kissed Rachel or become familiar with her body before that night; those are Bible standards.

Young people today listen with amazement to the story of Jacob and Rachel because they have accepted a different standard. They have accepted our culture's standard that justifies "petting" with many different partners before marriage. In shocking numbers, Christian young people have surrendered to cultural and peer pressure regarding their sexual standards. Their friends do it. Everyone does it. Why shouldn't they do it?

Another problem among Christians is that Bible literacy is at an all-time low. Neither parents nor children know the basic facts of the Bible. Most cannot support their beliefs as being founded in the Bible. Also, today many force the Bible to conform to their desires and to their lifestyles rather than submitting to the scriptural requirements of the Lord. Rather than searching for grounds to remain married, thousands of Christian couples now search the Bible to find support for getting a divorce because they "are not happy any more."

Changing a Culture

Pertaining to the matter of how to go about changing a culture, there are two other Christian camps that stand in opposition to each other. The first camp can be classified as the evangelicals, who still believe that the primary mission of the church is to enlarge the kingdom of God through the evangelization of the world. This camp promotes the salvation of the lost as primary. "Get them saved and get them out of the world," is their motto. They believe this is going to be the biblical means for changing the world. It would be difficult to argue with this viewpoint. However,

As Christians, we have looked into the face of our culture and become its mirror image.

if evangelism alone is supposed to change a culture, then something is wrong, for our culture is not being changed. It remains deteriorated. Modern evangelicalism in America has not had much of an impact on our culture.

The second camp tends to attract those who embrace a social ministry rather than using evangelism as their primary means of changing the world. Members of this camp believe that those who profess to be genuine Christians will be involved in the social issues that have destroyed our culture. They have shifted away from evangelism to social activism, and they maintain that "as they are going," they can effectively pursue justice and reach the lost as effectively as those who are looked upon as pure evangelicals. According to this group, the spiraling diseases of our sick society must be fought on the front lines of our society. They believe that evangelism occurs as they provide shelter for the homeless, support for life to the unborn, and food for the poor, and this is their remedy for our culture.

We must sound the alarm to parents who are raising their children in a culture that must be changed.

This book is not being written to take sides with either of the two camps. It is being written to sound the alarm to parents who are raising their children in a culture that must be changed. If you are an evangelical, then win souls with a zeal that will bring the lost into the kingdom of the Lord. If you embrace the concept of a social ministry, then care for the sick and feed the poor as you

44

seek to change the world. However, I prescribe a more specific and intensive method for parents.

While each of these camps has good points, it is imperative that perpetual, individual repentance, purification, and prayerfulness be practiced by both camps on an individual level. We will be ineffective in changing our culture until we do so. It is God alone who can send forth the tidal wave of His Spirit and bring about such a change that our culture itself will be changed, yet God will not move unless His children are walking in personal relationship with Him and caring for those whom He has sovereignly placed in our care: our own children and our families. We take the first step in the redemption of our culture by looking to ourselves and judging the intents of our hearts. We must ask ourselves, "Is the Lord truly the Lord of my life? Do I seek His will above all else?" If these things are true in our lives, we must then turn our attention toward the needs of our children and seek to lead them into a full and fruitful relationship with the Lord. If we win the whole world and yet lose our own children, what have we accomplished?

Churches and ministries are filled with leaders and individuals who actively promote either their evangelism or their social ministry, yet even as they minister, they remain personally dried up, empty vessels. Thousands of Christians go forth to minister while leaving behind homes that are not Christ centered. They seek to impart some spiritual gift to others while their children are being left to flounder beneath the overwhelming influence of our culture. God will not bless something in public that He cannot bless in private. Until our homes and individual lives are firmly established upon the Lord, we toil in vain to change our culture.

In order to change our culture, regardless of which of the two camps we agree with, we must begin by changing our individual lives and our homes. The task of redeeming a culture steeped in darkness may seem too large a task for the average Christian, but we can certainly redeem ourselves and our children, and our homes are the most likely place to succeed. By far the most influential instrument for accomplishing the redemption of our children is our parental example. In the next chapter, we will explore some of the things that we can begin to do to become living examples of God's truth in the eyes of our children.

IN SUMMARY

There are two schools of thought regarding the best way to redeem our culture. One believes we should "come out from among them" and therefore stays hidden behind the walls of the church. The other camp believes we should be "the light of the world" and go forth and shine before men.

Jesus taught His disciples to go into the world and be a counterculture to the corruption that was in the world and to have a different standard and values system than what the world promotes.

The church has become so immersed in the world that there is barely a distinction between the two. The church reflects the same lifestyles and morality as the world.

Even within the camp of Christians who believe

that we should go forth into the world as "lights," there is a division on how to go forth. One group believes in evangelism and the other group believes in social programs.

Changing our culture will come about through perpetual repentance, purification, and prayerfulness. We should beseech God through prayer to send His Spirit and bring about a change in our culture that will be a lasting change.

We take the first step in the redemption of our culture by looking to ourselves and judging the intents of our hearts and the goals of our lives.

In order to change our culture, we must begin by changing our individual lives and homes.

PART II
PRESCRIPTION FOR PARENTING

Chapter Four

Observation of Tradition

Deuteronomy chapter six details the Lord's commandment to Moses to write down and deliver a formula regarding the family. The principles contained in that formula were to be observed throughout succeeding generations. It is clear that the Jewish nation went beyond the boundaries of the traditions that God established for the sake of His people, adding their own man-made formulas. The result was ritualism, and there is a difference between tradition and ritualism. While tradition is vibrant and warm, ritualism is dry and impersonal. God knew the value of traditions and He gave them for the purpose of building and maintaining a strong sense of identity and to provide a link between Himself and His children and between the generations of mankind.

First, traditions help give us our identity. I remember learning as a young boy the tradition of going to church faithfully. In our home, everything always centered around our faith in God and our faithfulness to our church. We never asked our parents if we were going to attend church on Sunday morning, Sunday night or even Wednesday night because if church was in session, we were going to be there. We were not permitted to play sports on church nights or have employment that kept us from church. And this family tradition was never a topic for discussion; it was just something that we were taught by example from the day we were born. I also remember the Friday night tradition of going with my father to see the Cincinnati Reds play baseball at Crosley Field or to catch a high school football or basketball game. Also, we would always look forward to short trips to the country in Kentucky, just being together as a family, for a few days. The succulent smell of my mother's pumpkin pies started the traditional squabbling between my brother and me concerning who got the biggest piece. These traditions helped me build a solid identity as a member of my church and of my family. They were good traditions that helped me establish who I was, and today they keep me connected to my past. They were traditions in my childhood that provided examples for me as a parent to my own children.

Tradition keeps us connected to the past and to the future and helps to give us our identity.

Traditions give us an understanding of where we have come from, as individuals, as families, and as nations. They also give us a sense of being connected by allowing us to be a part of something that is bigger than we are and that has been handed down from generation to generation. Traditions keep us connected to the past and provide a gridwork for the future, and through the healing of family tradition, we can help break the generational curse brought upon our culture through the revolution of the '60s. We can stop the cycle that despises anything to do with the past, with tradition and with the establishment. We can do this by establishing some bearings of tradition within our own families.

In this effort to renew an appreciation for the importance of tradition in family life and its long-term effect upon our children, I am not advocating some dry, dull, empty forms of ritualism. Again, tradition and ritualism are two different things. But I am encouraging parents to begin to establish now some fundamental, meaningful activities that will be a connecting link between the past and the future for our children. And creating some traditions that will cement families together and reconnect them with biblical roots the way God intended will require some intentional planning and effort.

The dictionary defines tradition as "the practice of handing down information, stories, beliefs, and customs by word of mouth or by example from one generation to another without written instruction in order to establish and reinforce a strong sense of identity." As I have said, there is a distinct difference between tradition and ritual, although many people confuse the two. This is the dictionary's definition for ritual: "the order of words prescribed for a religious ceremony; a ceremonial act or action." Establishing family traditions is not to be looked upon as rigid ritualism that never changes. Contrary to that, traditions often need to be revised and reformed in order to keep them culturally relevant, as many modern Jewish families have done with their festivals. We must remember that the basic purpose for having traditions is to reinforce a strong sense of identity, and this is true for families and for nations. However, in order for traditions to fulfill their God-given purpose, they must be established with a right purpose in mind. The purpose God had in establishing traditions was to keep His people connected, as Jewish traditions kept God's people connected to Him, to the past of their ancestors and to the future of their children. If our traditions do not have the right purpose and support, they will end up becoming empty activities.

The Principle of Hearing, Loving and Teaching

Let's look at the principle supplied by the Lord in chapter six of Deuteronomy. These words were handed down to Moses from God, and they were intended to be an established custom or practice for the nation of Israel. The scene takes place as the children of Israel stand on the border of the Promised Land. In order to inherit what had been given to them by God, they needed to conquer a corrupt culture. Yet, even before they had completed their conquest, they were to abide by this principle which emphasizes three words: hear, love and teach. This was God's formula for his children:

> Hear, O Israel: The Lord our God is one Lord: And thou shalt love the LORD with all thine heart, and with all thy soul, and with all thy might. And these words which I command thee this day, shall be in thine heart: And thou shalt teach them diligently unto thy children, and shalt

talk of them when thou sittest in thine house, and when thou walkest by the way, and when thou liest down, and when thou risest up. And thou shalt bind them for a sign upon thine hand, and they shall be as frontlets between thine eyes. And thou shalt write them upon the door-posts of thy house, and on thy gates.[1]

Hear the Truth

First we are to hear one certain, unshakable truth: "Hear, O Israel: The LORD our God is one LORD." This means that we are to acknowledge the Lord's uniqueness as God and the essence of His unity within our families. Moses commanded the Israelites to repeat this as a statement of their faith. It is known as the Shema, and it is repeated thousands of times a day by Jews throughout the world.

Our children must certainly hear our statements about the Lord during times of His blessings upon our families, but they must also hear words of affirmation that He remains Lord even during seasons of family trials. When our children hear affirmation of God's sovereignty in both the easy times and in the hard times, this truth will be transferred to them. Also, it is obviously very important that our children see in our actions that we believe the words we speak.

Along with hearing words of affirmation about the Lord, children must receive verbal affirmation about them-selves. If children do not receive these endorsements of their self worth within the family, they may not hear them at all; we cannot depend upon the world to do this for them. God made both us and our children in His image, and he crafted into us to have a love for Him and the desire to enjoy a relationship with Him throughout eternity. Our children have eternal value, and it is important that they hear this from us on a continual basis.

One of the most effective means of counteracting the immoral influence of our culture upon our children is to instill in them a strong sense of their value, and God has established the family as the place to do this. Inside the protective walls of the family, we can build a strong sense of self worth and identity into our children. And one of the most helpful tools of the family in doing this is tradition. Parents need to establish a tradition of letting children hear about their self-worth and their value in the eyes of their parents and God.

One nonbelieving father went about establishing the tradition of sharing Friday-night dinners with his children. He insisted that the tablecloth be spread, the candles lit and cloth napkins be used. He saw to it that it was a leisurely, pleasurable time for all his children. On occasion he would bring small gifts to each of his children. He reserved these moments for telling about his own shortcomings and humorous moments as a child. But the most important thing he maintained during these Friday nights was the deliberate decision to let his children hear how pleased he was with them, how courageous he thought some of their actions had been and how maturely they were handling their weekly

Children can be extremely perceptive in distinguishing between the genuine and the counterfeit in adults.

allowances. There is much to be praised about a father who establishes a family tradition just for the sake of spending time with his children and his family, and while this man's example is admirable, the Christian father should go one step further. While undergirding the self-worth of our children, we should also establish traditions that reinforce God's truth in their lives.

One Christian mother established a tradition to honor her son's birthday by jotting down all the things the Lord had impressed upon her throughout the year. She not only jotted down her own impressions from the Lord, but she noted special moments and occasions when her son walked according to the truth revealed in the Scriptures. Before her son's birthday each year, she made a simple handwritten book of these impressions and presented it as a gift to her son. At the birthday celebration, she passed the book around to different family members who read aloud what she had written. The son glowed beneath the words he heard from his family. Throughout the years, this simple book remained her son's favorite gift. She had begun a tradition by which her son heard about his value and the faithfulness of God in his life. Upon his entering his teen years, the mother believed he would look upon the simple handmade book as childish so she skipped making it one year. As a testimony to the value of such traditions, the son protested loudly and insisted the book was very special to him.

There is also another perspective on the word "hear" that we must consider. Parents who are determined to redeem their children must also practice "hearing." Parents need to hear what their teenage children are saying as they live before them. It takes courage to be vulnerable before our children, and it must be approached with humility. We must also have the maturity and integrity not to hold our children in bondage because of what they say to us. We must commit ourselves to spending some private and uninterrupted time with our children and asking them questions about ourselves. And then we must hear, really hear, what they are saying. They must have the liberty to be honest with us, and under these circumstances, most children will generally open up and "tell it like they see it." Consequently, we must be prepared to come tumbling down from our pedestals of spirituality. A teenage son might question why his dad teaches the children in a Sunday school class about prayer and reading the Bible when he has not allowed his son to see that he prays or reads his Bible at home. A daughter may ask her mother why she condemns people who do not know the Lord without ever having witnessed to one of those lost souls. It takes a brave heart to hear such things and make a change as a result, but it is an important part of "hearing."

Love the Lord God

The second instrument in God's formula given to Moses in Deuteronomy was love. There was more in God's command to love the Lord God "with all your heart and with all your soul and with all your might" than just some ego-maniacal deity sitting on a throne in heaven demanding that everyone love Him. God knew that it would be love for Him that would carry the children of Israel through all that was in store for them both as individuals and as a nation. And not only would this unequivocal love for Him carry them through what was ahead of them, but the depth of their love for Him would be transferred to their children. The Lord commanded fervency here. He knew it would be this inflamed, all-consuming love for Him that would keep them intact as a nation. It is also what cements our families together.

It is impossible for me to transfer to my children a love for the Lord that I do not personally possess. It has been proven that men can preach the gospel, endure the ministry and maintain positions of authority without a love for the Lord, but no parent can transfer a love for the Lord to his child unless he embraces it himself. Children can be extremely perceptive in distinguishing between the genuine and the counterfeit in adults. If I tell my children not to steal and they watch me knowingly keep the two extra dollars mistakenly given to me by the grocery store clerk, then everything I have said about honesty falls to the ground. If I do not allow my children to speak profanity and yet I angrily curse at the man who pulls his car into the lane in front of me, then, again my words fall to the ground. My example before my children will shout volumes.

For our children to follow the Lord throughout the length of their days, there must be instilled within them a passionate and intimate relationship with the Lord.

We know that true Christianity is a relationship and not just a religion. We have been taught that it is love for the Lord that forms the foundation for that relationship. However, if the love for the Lord is not clearly evident in a parent's life, then he must cry out for God to reveal Himself. Upon God's revelation of Himself, that parent will fall immediately in love with Him.

And if a parent's love for the Lord has lost its fire, then he must cry out for Him to rekindle that passion. If our children are to follow the Lord throughout the length of their days, they must be infused with a passionate and intimate relationship with the Lord God, Jehovah. Before we can ever pass such a desire for the Lord along to our children, they must witness it in our personal lives; it must be lived out before them in our homes.

But how do we begin to foster this relationship with the Lord in our own lives? We begin with prayer. We cry out to Him to reveal Himself to us, and then we diligently seek Him and continue to seek Him until we have felt the touch of His hand upon our lives. We must beseech God to bathe us in His repentance and rekindle that fire for Him within our hearts. These prayers from His children are not ignored by the Lord. More than we desire this relationship with Him, He desires it. He yearns to spend time with us, and once we have touched the hem of His garment, we will repeat what the two disciples said after spending time with Him on the road to Emmaus after His resurrection: "Did not our heart burn within us, while He talked with us by the way...."[2]

As we seek to establish our families upon a foundation of genuine love, the one thing that will never fail, we must base that love upon a love relationship with the Lord. Once the foundations are correct in our personal lives and in our homes, then we stand in the gap and redeem a culture that has gone haywire.

Teach Them Diligently

Although Chapter 5 details the objectives in training our children, I will briefly mention the following with regard to teaching as one of God's principles for our children. The scriptures exhort us in this way:

> And thou shalt teach them diligently unto thy children, and shalt talk of them when thou sittest in thine house, and when thou walkest by the way, and when thou liest down, and when thou risest up. And thou shalt bind them for a sign upon thine hand, and they shall be as frontlets between thine eyes. And thou shalt write them upon the doorposts of thy house, and on thy gates.[3]

Teaching is not an option for parents. It is mandatory and comes along as part of the privilege of being a parent. The responsibility for educating children in things of the Lord has always belonged to the home and not to some institution or to professional teachers or preachers. The Hebrew word indicates that teaching is "repeating," telling something over and over again. Charles Swindoll makes this astute observation and comment about how we are to be "diligent" in the teaching of our children:

> The word "diligently" in English is actually an adverb, but in Hebrew the root term is a verb that means "to sharpen." So if read literally, the statement would be: "...and you shall sharpen your sons." The New International Version doesn't miss it by far when it renders the verse, "You shall impress them on your children." The term appears in a particular stem in the Hebrew language that adds intensity to the verb. "You shall intensely sharpen your sons." It's a strong command. So it isn't a passive action: it is a very

aggressive and assertive involvement in the educational process–all within a family setting."[4]

Swindoll goes on to say that one of the big mistakes made by parents is assuming that their children will "automatically capture our zeal for Christ."[5] This is why it is so important that God has written down His principle for teaching our children in His Word. Swindoll likens the process to an "automatic training session."[6]

The Hebrews had a term for making a formal proclamation, in delivering a lecture. It is not used here. There's also a term for just talking. That's the one used here. That is extremely significant! We are to talk of spiritual things just as we would talk about anything else in our home. You talk together about how the Dodgers played last night. No big deal, you just talk about that. You talk about what you're going to do next week. You simply talk about it. You talk about the pressure you felt today from so-and-so. You talk about what you're going to have for supper. You may talk about what you plan to watch on television that evening. You don't hold classes on it, you merely talk about it. There is an easy-going, natural flow of conversation. That's the word used here. That is what will make your Christianity authentic. It isn't a Sunday lifestyle! It is a Monday, Tuesday, Wednesday, Thursday, Friday, Saturday, Sunday, Monday, Tuesday, and on and on in the cycle-of-living lifestyle. So much so, that Christ fits naturally into the regular conversation and lifestyle of the home.[7]

So, as we go about establishing traditions, we would be wise to build upon the three words of hear, love, and teach with regard to our families. In Proverbs 24:3-4, we are told, "By wisdom a house is built, and by understanding it is established; and by knowledge the rooms are filled with all precious and pleasant riches." If we are going to be wise, then we will build according to God's principles. And His formula for linking the generations is to hear, love and teach.

Unfortunately, people do not go to college or attend schools where they can earn degrees on how to become parents. People generally become the same kind of parents as their parents were to them because we normally learn parenting by example only. Few make the effort to come out from under the misguided examples of their own parents and try to establish a new heritage of parenting for their children. And the few who make that choice will admit that there is a price to pay. The cost for following Jesus does not come about by simply talking about Him. It involves laying down one's life on a daily basis in order to follow the Lord and to establish a personal relationship with Him. It means daily walking as a true disciple of Christ.

Making Traditions

You may be thinking that you are not creative enough to go about establishing family traditions in your home that would include hearing, loving, and teaching, and it is true that some may be more adept at doing this than others. However, Christian bookstores are filled with books that can spark ideas for establishing special family traditions. We just have to keep in mind that the purpose for these traditions is to stay connected to God and past and future generations, and to authenticate a strong identity for our children. Also, we must remember to employ the three key words of hearing, loving, and teaching our children. And when we use books as aids, we don't have to feel constrained to copy an exact formula. Rather, we should use them as springboards from which to develop your own family traditions.

Jewish traditions normally encompass two broad areas, events and stories. The first event that God instructed the Jewish people to establish as a traditional festival was the Passover. This event of the Passover became the birth canal through which Israel was born as a nation. It celebrates the Exodus of the Israelites from Egypt. This first event that was to be established as a tradition for the children of Israel carried a "from generation to generation" concept. Jewish tradition today teaches that this firstborn of Jewish festivals contains the character of Jewish memory. They believe that as a people they are commanded to recall the past in order to live well in the present and maintain a view of their future.

In addition to this actual event, the Jewish people were commanded to tell the story of Exodus. Still today they believe that telling the story was commanded of them by God not simply to cause them to remember the Exodus but to enable them to expand upon the tale, to explore its complexities and to develop its meaning. The Haggadah, the liturgy used by the Jews at Passover, states:

> In every generation, each person should feel as though she or he were redeemed from Egypt, as it is said: "You shall tell your children on that day saying, It is because of what the Lord did for me when I went free out of Egypt." For the Holy One redeemed not only our ancestors; He redeemed us with them.[8]

The uniqueness of Passover to the Jewish people is that

they recognize it as an event in which they participated and in which they continue to participate. They believe it to be their own story, not just some ancient history that they retell every year at Passover.

It is interesting to study the traditions that have arisen among the Jews regarding Passover. Although unregenerate Jews ignorantly "act out" the gospel every year through their traditions, to those who know Christ it is a clear picture of His redemption. As Christians we often look toward the Jewish community with condescension and arrogance because we feel that we have accepted the real truth regarding the Messiah. And this is true. It is a fact that most Jewish people have been blinded to the truth about Jesus. We, the Gentile church, however, are blinded to the truth of tradition and its God-given purpose to link us from "generation to generation" and thereby give us a strong identity as the people of God. Again, I am not speaking of ritualism, but of the value of traditions. These traditional "festivals" given by God to the Jewish nation were meant to be road maps for the Jews.

One can say that the festivals act as lodgings for travelers making their way through the year. These festival inns provide special accommodations not solely for rest or retreat from the world, but also places to halt and take our bearings to make sure we are traveling and not just going around in circles. These are inns not for sleeping but rather for awakening from obliviousness.[9]

Observance of traditions has been imbedded into the Jewish culture for centuries. These traditions are a vital element of Jewish identity. They are looked upon as being "special accommodations" to awaken them from oblivion that settles in so easily throughout the year. Passover has the "built-in monitor" that guarantees the story of the Exodus will be repeated on a yearly basis in that it involves a rehearsing of the reason for the tradition. How often have we celebrated one of our traditional festivals, such as Thanksgiving, only to realize later that we were so concerned about the turkey and dressing that we failed to "give thanks to God" as a family? This is one reason why the purpose behind the tradition is so important. If the original purpose of Thanksgiving was to give thanks, then we need to re-establish that purpose. We need to begin some traditions that insure that we remember to give thanks. Our children will love this, and they will carry these traditions into their adult lives.

There are several big "events" that arise in our lives on an annual basis like Thanksgiving, Christmas, Easter and Independence Day. These events can be instrumental in creating cherished traditions in our families. But in addition to these events, it is essential for us to come up with some special times that are for our families exclusively. Many have employed the "family night" with great success. Others have had special "dates" with their children on a one-on-one basis. Some have begun to celebrate the spiritual "birthdays" for their children with the same fanfare that they celebrate natural birthdays. And, of course, many families do have an on-going tradition of telling family stories on Thanksgiving with the intent of teaching thankfulness and gratitude for past ancestors.

I know of a grandmother who faithfully took pictures of all her grandchildren throughout the Christmas holidays. She carefully preserved the pictures in individual albums for each grandchild. On one page of the album, she kept a journal of that grandchild's personal actions and reactions to Christmas that year, of visiting relatives, of parties and special events and of gifts. When the albums were completed after Christmas each year, the grandmother set them aside in a closet without showing the pictures to her grandchildren. When the next Christmas rolled around, the grandmother would bring out the albums and view them with her grandchildren. Precious moments of laughter and tears would ensue during those times shared between the grandmother and her grandchildren.

Along with the pictures and the journals, this wise grandma also recorded scriptural blessings and promises for each individual grandchild. She considered those blessings and promises as her spiritual gifts to her grandchildren. When she viewed the albums with her grandchildren, she told them about the Scriptures she believed the Lord had impressed her to pray for them that past year. This was a grandmother's contribution to starting a family tradition. She established a family tradition that included both events and stories. The event was Christmas and the stories revolved around her grandchildren's Christmases throughout their lives and the promises from the Lord regarding her grandchildren. And her grandchildren heard. They knew they were loved. And they were taught. This grandmother understood that she was an ancestral link for her grandchildren. What she did may reach forward three, four or perhaps five generations.

Establishing traditions does not guarantee that our children will not be influenced by the culture in which we live; however, if they are created and maintained genuinely and faithfully, then they can become those places to halt and take our bearings to make sure we are traveling and not just going around in circles.

IN SUMMARY

God gave Moses a formula regarding the family, and He commanded that the principles contained within that formula be observed throughout all generations.

The Lord knew that the value of traditions was for building and for maintaining a strong sense of identity. They were ordained to link His children to Himself throughout the generations.

Tradition has a long-term effect upon our children. It can be instrumental in pulling the family unit back to its roots as God established it.

There is a difference between tradition and ritual. Tradition is the practice of handing down information, stories, beliefs and customs by word of mouth or by example from one generation to another in order to reinforce a strong sense of identity. Ritual is a ceremonial act or action.

In God's formula for the family, He stressed hearing, loving and teaching. Our children need to hear the Word of God. They need to hear how we love them. And it is our responsibility as parents to diligently teach our children.

If we need help in thinking up and establishing traditions in our homes, we can find it in numerous good Christian books that are on the market.

The Jewish people used events and stories to help instruct their children. The observance of their traditions has been imbedded into the Jewish culture for centuries and has been instrumental in helping them to maintain their identity.

Chapter Five

Objectives in Training
SECTION 1: Spiritual Legacy

helves in Christian bookstores are filled with books on the family. Scores of authors have written on the subject of children and how to train them up in the Lord. This chapter is not intended to duplicate what has already been written; rather, it is intended to jostle your memory and gently remind you of what you probably already know. If your family has made a wrong turn, this book will hopefully be a road map to guide you back to the King's highway. This chapter, however, does not deal with the heartbreaking experience of the prodigal. That issue is covered in a later chapter. This and the next four chapters deal primarily with ways to "bend the twig" in the direction it should grow.

Our first objectives in training are grouped under three categories: spiritual objectives, emotional objectives and social objectives. Ecclesiastes 4:12 refers to "A threefold cord [that] is not quickly broken," and every child should be trained in these three essential areas of life, the spiritual, emotional and social. Woven together, these three separate strands can form an unbreakable bond of identity and security for a child. By concentrating on these areas, a parent secures for his child a "cord that is not quickly broken." Each of these separate strands represents a firm objective within itself, but tied together they can provide a strong foundation, equipping a child to resist the influences of our culture. To a great degree, these three areas are interrelated and depend upon each other, yet we will discuss them as individual components in the building of a child's character. These three objectives then, the spiritual, the emotional and the social, will be referenced as the three-fold cord.

The objective of giving our children a spiritual, an emotional, and a social legacy forms a three-fold cord that is not easily broken.

Two other objectives, physical and moral training, that are as vitally important in the training objectives of our children, will be discussed in the next chapter. I will briefly mention them here in order to lay a proper foundation for the set of legacies I will be discussing. These two areas are also entwined because of the sexual content involved in the physical and moral training, yet there is more involved in the moral training of our children than just the sexual. As we add on these two final areas of the physical and the moral, the metaphor will change from the three-fold cord to an analogy of constructing a building.

Seeking to build character into the life of a child can parallel the construction of a building. A building consists of two main parts. The part below the ground is called the substructure or the foundation. The part above the ground is the superstructure. The foundation, or the substructure, is the structure that supports a building, as well as any of the occupants, furniture or equipment that may be moved either in or out of the building. Before anything can be built, there must first be a foundation upon which it can rest. It is interesting that there are three different types of foundations upon which buildings are erected: spread, pile, and pier.[1] I suggest that the three different types of foundations are parallel to the three different foundations that we must build in the substructure of our children's lives. The spiritual, the emotional and the social are absolute substructures or foundations upon which to build a child's character. These three areas are critical to a child's development.

Often we concentrate solely upon the superstructure, or the physical, that is above the ground in our children's lives. The physical and moral elements of a child's life are absolute necessities and should be addressed, but not to the neglect of the other three. These five "legacies" which we desire to impart to our children are all essential and are actually interrelated. Children must be fed. They must be bathed. They must exercise to develop healthy bodies. They must learn to possess their bodies as temples of the Holy Spirit and make right moral choices. Yet we begin with the substructure, the foundation, those things that are unseen and that will support our children's lives. If we attend to these substructures in the lives of our children, they will grow tall and beautiful from within and not just biologically. We must go down deep and build these foundations for them. Again, the three different sub-structures, or foundations, we need to build for our children are the spiritual, emotional, and social. With these elements, we build in the lives of our children the super-structure, that which is most clearly seen by the world, that part of the building that is above the ground. These five legacies will prove to be of more worth than silver and gold in the lives of our children.

What are the most influential ways in which parents can prepare their children for life in a disintegrating society? In order to discuss that, we need to begin with the two most influential factors in any child's life, Mom and Dad. In the Jewish tradition, children were usually left under the nurturing care of their mothers until the ages of five and seven years. Then the sons, primarily, were given over to the total care and influence of the father.

I have not heard this aphorism for years now, but when I was growing up, I used to hear it all the time: "The hand that rocks the cradle rules the world." That saying sum-marized our society's estimation of a mother's influence. Even in today's world, there is nothing more powerful or more influential than the role that a mother plays in the lives of her children. Whether it is a positive or a nega-tive influence, a mother's role produces a powerful per-suasion over the lives of her children. A mother's words, love and example follow all of us into adulthood, and the memory of her presence lasts throughout our lives. Those who were blessed with godly mothers, know that there is no substitute for what they impart into our lives.

Abraham Lincoln once said, "No one is poor who had a godly mother."

Most mothers begin to nurture their children even from within their womb. They feel them move within, and their hearts beat in tandem. They love them before they first hear their cries in the world. Upon giving birth, mothers cradle their babies, whisper secrets, sing lullabies, nurse and cuddle them in their protective arms. In families, it is generally the mother who provides transparent tenderness and unselfish love.

It is the father, on the other hand, who generally supplies leadership and security for his children. One of the greatest needs in the body of Christ today is for men who are decisive and strong-hearted, men who are not afraid to assume positions of leadership and who can stand firm in their convictions even when the going gets tough. These are the masculine qualities that reproduce themselves in younger boys who hunger for heroes after which to model themselves. Even as mothers generally provide the transparent tenderness for their children, fathers should provide transparent leadership for their children. Fathers who are open and vulnerable are actually capable of giving great security to their children. One of the accusations hurled against the fathers of the '50s was that they were never transparent before their children. Those fathers feared losing the respect of their children and ultimately lost their children to the '60s because of their failure to be transparent with

> *No one is poor who had a godly mother."*
>
> *-Abraham Lincoln*

them. Fathers who are willing to admit their failures and seek forgiveness receive greater respect from their children than those who try to cover themselves behind an impenetrable shield of silence or masculine authority.

Regarding the objective of a spiritual legacy, I will not be repeating the tried-and-true formulas for raising children. I am assuming that you already know about these principles and have hopefully already sewn them into the fabric of your children's lives. Instead, we will be looking at the objective of a spiritual legacy that is primarily established through the actions and attitudes of parents.

Objectives of a Spiritual Legacy

I begin with the spiritual objectives because the spiritual is the most vital of the strands in our three-fold cord. Statistics prove that even in Christian homes, most parents ignore the spiritual development of their children. Why is this? As parents, we must take a serious inventory of our own spiritual lives. Do we measure our behavior by the standards of Scripture or by what everyone else is doing? Do our children hear us talk about God in a personal and intimate manner? Are they witnessing an authentic walk of faith in our daily lives? It is important to begin this section on training children in spiritual objectives by focusing on the parents rather than the children because parents are the ultimate molders of the spiritual outlook of their children. Without any doubt, the church and Christian schools can give children facts about the Lord and the Bible. It is also true, however, that a child's spiritual outlook or his world view (how he views the world in which he lives) is taught by his parents' example in the home. If we are to fulfill our God-given purposes as parents, then it is essential that we leave our children with a strong spiritual legacy. One of the greatest things involved in a spiritual legacy is a spiritual world view, and this world view is taught in the home by the parents.

Before going any further, let me state that a spiritual legacy is not merely attending church or memorizing scripture. Both of these are important and contribute to a firm foundation, but neither of these should be the objective of a spiritual legacy.

With regard to spiritual objectives in the training of children, hitting the bull's eye is of utmost importance, and the arrow that will hit that target is one comprised of your proper actions and attitudes. Children are influenced more by a parent's actions and attitudes than by any amount of church attendance or even scores of memory verses. Also, reaching the objective of leaving a spiritual legacy does not happen overnight. It takes years of sacrificial and consistent effort to hit that bull's eye. It takes commitment from parents to walk daily as role models to their children. We model the unseen realities of the spiritual world for our children in our actions whether we realize we are doing it or not, so commitment to that is vital in a child's life.

Children are influenced more by the actions and attitudes of their parents in the home than by any amount of church attendance.

Many parents do not recognize the spiritual component that operates within their children from a very young age. Waiting until our children are "old enough to understand" is unscriptural and unwise. I can offer one certain promise on this issue: the Devil will not wait for our children to understand before he begins cultivating his plan to destroy them. As we have been sitting placidly in our pews with folded hands and depending on the Sunday school class to do our teaching job for us, the Devil has slipped in the back doors of our homes and shot his fiery darts into an entire generation of young children with the goal of destroying them. We cannot let this happen to our children!

> *The devil slipped in the back doors of our homes and shot his fiery darts into an entire generation of young children with the goal of destroying them.*

I believe that Christian schools and churches are responsible to do nothing more than undergird and confirm what we as parents have taught and what we live in front of our children. For years, I have told parents that people can listen and learn or they can live and learn. To listen and learn from those who have experienced things before us is a far better method. If we cannot control a child at age 2, then we don't have a prayer of controlling him at the age of 12. Training for children, both through the spoken word and through the lives we live before them, should begin the day they are born and remain consistent throughout their upbringing. As a father, I have told my daughters that dating is not even a consideration until they are sixteen years old, and perhaps not even at the age of sixteen. I have a better chance of influencing my girls early so that it doesn't become a point of controversy later. Also, it is important that rules be clearly defined and that consequences be defined so that when rules are broken, the child is not taken off guard by the consequences for his or her actions.

God gave us the responsibility for protecting our children and for giving them a spiritual legacy. It is our duty to begin to pray over them when they are infants; it is imperative that we beseech the Lord early for His wisdom regarding how to recognize the gifts and abilities that He has deposited in our little ones so that we can "bend the twig" in that direction. We must remember also that the parental blessing is a powerful weapon against spiritual forces. Before they even learn to crawl, we must vocally bless our children, asking the Lord to give them eyes to see Him, ears to hear Him and a heart that always seeks Him.

Hearing From God

There are several components that will strengthen any spiritual legacy, but the most vital of these is teaching a child how to hear from the Lord. Hearing from the Lord is not reserved for young people, adults and the elderly. Young children can and must learn to hear from the Lord. As parents, we must acknowledge that God is interested in developing a relationship with our children while they are still children. If we are to leave a spiritual legacy that will carry our children into their old age, then we need to carefully watch for the Lord to make a connection with them when they are children. We cannot afford to limit their connection to the Lord with simple bedtime prayers and reading them Bible story books. The story of Samuel verifies that God does communicate with young children, and we must recognize the hand of the Lord if He begins to communicate with our children.

The background of the story in I Samuel 3 is that there was a spiritual famine in the land. It was a rare thing at that time in Israel to receive a word or a vision from the Lord. It was in the midst of this dearth that the Lord sovereignly chose to reveal Himself and His word to the young boy, Samuel. The voice of the Lord came to Samuel two times while he was sleeping. Samuel mistakenly thought it was Eli who called out to him, so he ran to Eli's room. On two separate occasions, Eli told Samuel that he had not called him so Samuel returned to his bed. Upon the third time that Samuel heard the voice and again ran to Eli, the old priest finally understood what was going on. Eli realized that the Lord was the one Who had called out to Samuel. He instructed the young boy to listen. He told Samuel to go lie down and if he heard the voice again to say, "Speak, Lord; for thy servant heareth."

Eli was wise enough to realize what was happening between Samuel, as a child, and the Lord. As parents we must intuitively acknowledge that the Lord seeks to speak to our children. Just as we are a spiritual beings, so are our children. We must not rob them of hearing from the Lord or ignore the truth that God desires to communicate with them. It is our responsibility as parents to watch for these moments in our children's lives, even when they are quite young.

Learning God's Ways

In addition to hearing from the Lord, another objective

of providing a spiritual legacy for our children should be to teach them God's ways. Sunday schools across America do a superb job of teaching our children all about God, but few can teach His ways. This is because knowing God's ways comes from intimate revelation of Him on a personal level. When a child learns the ways of God, then he is on the threshold of entering into the rich storehouse of God's wisdom.

Moses cried out for the Lord, "Show me Your ways." He had known all about God from the plagues in Egypt, but now he cried out to know God's ways. He wanted to know more about God's habits, His customs, His methods and His manners of dealing with people. Moses had experienced deliverance along with almost three million other Israelites, but he was not satisfied to stop there. He wanted to know God's ways of deliverance. He wanted to know God's ways of leading. Perhaps this was because Moses had experienced a taste of God's ways with the Red Sea in front of him and Pharaoh's army behind him. He experienced that God's way of deliverance on that day was to get him into an impossible position, penned in between two destructive forces. Then God miraculously opened up the Red Sea. Even after the events that had transpired in Egypt and the Red Sea, Moses hungered to know God's ways, and the result of this hunger to know God and His ways was that Moses' face shone so brightly he had to cover it when he was with the children of Israel.

Few of our children will likely ever be called upon by God to deliver an entire nation from bondage. And their faces may never shine so brightly that they have to cover them with veils. But if they experience God's ways in their lives as young children, the chances of their straying as teenagers will be less likely. If a child feels the touch of the Lord's hand upon his life as a young child and experiences the Lord's presence at an early age, he may never be faced with the question for which many teenagers struggle to find an answer: "What's the point of it all?" It is only when they find no answer to this important question that our young people stray away from the church and end up with the secular world view of "Live and let live; and live as comfortably as possible while you are at it."

I want to stress again that we parents need to evaluate our own lives regarding the above spiritual objectives as a prerequisite to equipping our children. Do *we* hear the Lord's voice? Do *we* know the Lord's ways? Have *we* experienced the glory of His presence in the private moments of our time spent with Him? If our answers are negative, then how can we teach our children the ways of the Lord?

A Pure Conscience

A child's conscience is God's gift of a warning signal to him, and every child is born with one. Wise parents will take the conscience into consideration in the raising of their children. Although a child's conscience is his sovereign possession, his parents can help to create an atmosphere in his home in which the child's conscience can learn to be strong, pure and assured of its salvation.

When our children were born into our families, they knew nothing about the language we spoke, the culture into which they were born, the church we attended or our values system. They came into this world knowing nothing, and they know nothing in those initial years except what they learn from us. The responsibility of raising that child so that he makes the right moral choices in life is a demanding task, and fulfilling this responsibility necessitates the guarding of our children's consciences when they are young.

The Bible is our handbook for life, and it possesses the wealth and wisdom of Almighty God. Because of the fact that the Bible is the greatest source of training material for our children, it is very important that parents become students of the Bible. How can we ever transfer the wisdom of God to our children if we ourselves are not students of His Word?

I look for every opportunity in daily life to share a biblical principle or scriptural lesson with my children. Years ago when I was driving down the road with my daughter, Heather, we saw a man dressed in tattered clothes, walking along the road pushing a shopping cart. The shopping cart contained all of that man's worldly goods. Heather commented, "Look at that poor man, Daddy." I took that opportunity to discuss with her the possibility that he may have made a series of bad decisions and that he may be living out the consequences of the bad decisions that he made. But then I went on to say that we were to have compassion on that man because if it were not for the grace of God and our decision to live by His principles, we might be the ones pushing the grocery cart and he could be the one driving the car.

The overflow of wisdom from the Word of God is waiting to be shared with our children on a daily basis through the life lessons that God makes available to us. There are very few families today that have either the time or the resources to sit down collectively at the end of the day and open their Bibles and share a time of devotions. However, we do not have to be defeated. God grants us opportunities every day to share with our children some scriptural principles that are in His written Word. I remember one of my daughters discussing the unfairness of playing on a volleyball team. I took that opportunity to teach her that life is not always fair. If we get what is fair, we get Hell. I am glad that God operates on the basis of mercy rather than fairness.

The Bible describes several different types of consciences: weak, pure, defiled and seared. We want to learn how to keep our children's consciences pure, but we must slip on velvet gloves of intuitive compassion when we deal with these fragile aspects of our offspring. The goal is to help them develop a strong conscience because a weak conscience can be a spiritual liability. Those who have a weak conscience tend to consider themselves as being super spiritual, but in reality they are the very opposite. These people tend to be legalistic in their outlook and can be overly critical of others. Rather than being mature spiritually, people with weak consciences are actually immature, and they reveal this in their legalism. As parents, our goal is not to be legalistic as we deal with our children. And in order to avoid it, we must carefully tend our own consciences and maintain spiritual strength. As we do this, we can guide our children in the steps of spiritual maturity.

Confess and Forsake All Known Sin

There are several principles that are involved in keeping a pure conscience. The first one is to confess and to forsake all known sin. Obviously, there will be times when we do not realize that our child has sinned, so we will not be able to guide him into the confession of that sin. There will be those times, however, when we see that sin has entered into his life. Are we to point our finger of condemnation? Should we depend upon the law of consequences to take over as a result of his sin? Or should we issue corporal punishment? Naturally, how we handle disobedience or transgression is as unique as each parenting couple; however, we must always carefully observe our child after we administer correction. We should look for evidence of conviction and contrition that indicates his conscience is working, and if we observe it, we should use this time as a valuable opportunity to teach him the principle of confession and forsaking known sin. And it is important we do this with a spirit of humility and with the loving support of the Scriptures which pertain to confessing sin.

An excellent verse for dealing with this issue is I John 1:9, which deals with confession of sin and God's provision for it in the Christian life. When we are bearing our hearts and admitting guilt, it is very important to know that "if we confess our sins, He is faithful and righteous to forgive us our sins and to cleanse us from all unrighteousness." Also, it is helpful to know that we are not alone. As a parent, you may wish to share with your child how you at one time sinned and had to cling to the verse in James 5:16 that says, "Therefore, confess your sins to one another, and pray for one another, so that you may be healed." This process educates a child's conscience by teaching it to focus on the true knowledge of God's revealed truth, an important process covered in Chapter 2. The conscience operates based upon knowledge, and when our children sin, we must help them obtain knowledge of the truth by pointing them to

God's Word. This will strengthen their consciences and help them to stay pure.

Making Restitution

Along with confessing sin, there is another principle that is necessary to maintain a pure conscience. It is restitution. If a child commits a sin against another person, then his parents must help him to keep his conscience pure by walking him through the principle of restitution. For example, if a child is caught lying, cheating or stealing, then he must make restitution. If his parents will guide him firmly through this process, they will assist him in maintaining a pure conscience. This may seem harsh, but is God's way and His commandment in both the Old and the New Testaments (Numbers 5:6-7; Philemon 19; Luke 19:8). But we must watch ourselves, as well. It is difficult for a parent to insist that his children return a bar of candy that he stole from the grocery store, if he has seen his parent take towels from the hotel room where they spent their last vacation.

If we choose not to do things God's way, then we rip a hole in the fabric of the spiritual legacy we seek to impart to them.

An important point about demanding restitution is that it is not a matter of legalism, and it is not meant to embarrass or humiliate the child or anyone else involved. We need to go to all this trouble in order to protect the purity of our children's consciences. We do this by walking through the process of admitting to a wrong and then paying the price for that wrong, whether it be a simple apology or the replacement of a possession or some other type of restitution. The idea is that we teach them that if we choose to neglect a commandment of God, we damage ourselves or others and then we must make that situation right.

Our actions and our attitudes in these situations teach our children about our own personal values system and moral beliefs much more clearly than our words. As surely as the sun rises in the morning, these values will be imparted to our children. We can ignore little Johnny's theft because it is only a fifty-cent piece of candy, but the lesson we are teaching him is penetrating his very soul. When he hears us talk about honesty, he may not say anything, but inside he will realize that we only talk about it; we do not walk it out in our own lives. The reason I would encourage a parent to go to the trouble and embarrassment of taking Johnny back to the store to pay for the candy bar is because this would help to keep his conscience pure before God. And to Johnny's parents, his character should be worth the trouble. The formation of his character should be worth the embarrassment.

Asking Forgiveness

The third principle of a pure conscience is asking forgiveness and being reconciled with the person who has been wronged. Most parents themselves put off dealing with this issue in their own lives. They somehow believe that procrastination will silence their conscience, but it does not. If we parents are walking in forgiveness, it is much easier for us to watch over our children and help them to do the same. The operation of this principle in a child's life will reach far into the future. One of the foundational problems in the body of Christ today is that many people harbor unforgiveness in their hearts toward others. It is essential that we not only walk in forgiveness but that we teach our children to do likewise.

The Lord said, "If you forgive men for their transgressions, your heavenly Father will also forgive you. But if you do not forgive men, then your Father will not forgive your transgressions."[2] Christians try to skirt this verse or ignore it entirely, yet the Scriptures clearly state that if we do not forgive men for what they do to us, then the Father will not forgive us. We cannot neglect teaching our children this vital truth. Other than hearing the voice of the Lord, walking in forgiveness is probably the most important aspect of a spiritual legacy we leave to our children.

Monitoring our children's consciences in these three principles is serious business. It must be done in a spirit of humility, and we must model it carefully in our own lives before we can expect if from our children. Our children learn much more readily from the personal examples they see in our lives than they do from church attendance or even from memorizing Scriptures. We must saturate our children's consciences with the Word of God not only by requiring that they memorize God's Word but by modeling it for them. Then, when situations arise in our families, we can focus on the realities of God's triumphant grace in our lives. We must prayerfully ask the Lord to give us wisdom as we teach our children to subject their consciences to the truth of God and the teachings revealed in the Scriptures about a pure conscience. Once a child's conscience becomes clearly focused, it will give him the clear feedback that he needs to keep him away from sin. We must keep our minds focused on the necessity of training our children to hear the voice of the Lord, learn the ways of the Lord and maintain a pure conscience before the Lord.

Now we must acknowledge a valid question: What about children who were not taught these three principles as little children and are now teenagers? Obviously, it is best to teach these principles early, but they can be applied at anytime during a child's life. God is capable of changing the character of anyone regardless of age, and it is never too late for any parent or his child. Establishing a spiritual legacy for teenagers may have to be approached a little differently than when they were younger, but nothing is impossible with the Lord.

We must keep our minds focused on the necessity of training our children to hear the voice of the Lord, in learn the ways of the Lord and in maintain a pure conscience.

Many parents may be dismayed because they realize that America's culture has already manifested itself in the character of their child. Most Christian teenagers today have embraced a secular values system rather than one that is based upon the Bible. The majority has shifted toward the world's attitude regarding their behavior, their dress and their morals. More and more, Christian youth are sexually active; almost yearly, Christian schools see their female students dropping out because they are pregnant. Teenage pregnancy is prevalent among teens who were raised in church. Cheating in Christian schools is as prevalent as

it is in a public school. Students in private Christian schools are as insolent and disrespectful to authority as those who do not profess to know the Lord. It is clear that there has been a notable shift in values and behavior among our Christian young people. Yet these same teenagers go to church on Sunday and speak the same language of spirituality as the adults. We have somehow taught our teenagers to memorize all of the facts in the Bible without thinking like a true disciple of Christ. They have somehow missed out on the connection between those Bible facts and the inherent moral truth that is revealed in the Scriptures. They fail to see that the Scriptures have authority over every aspect of their lives simply because God Himself is the Author of the moral truth inherently found in the Bible.

In other words, young people do not have a Christian perspective or view the world through the lens of the Scriptures. They do not view the world the way Christ viewed it. While many believe that having a secular world view is not very likely for Christian children, this has proven to be false. The fact is that our children will either view their world through secular eyes or through Biblical eyes. They will either accept the secular world's values system or they will accept God's values system, and assuming that they will see the world God's way just because their parents are Christians and they attend church themselves is folly. One only needs to consider the young people in his own church or Christian school to verify this. The majority of them do not think like Christians. They do not view the world from a Christian perspective. And the reason for this is primarily that their parents failed to give them a spiritual legacy.

A Christian world view is essential in any spiritual legacy, and it should be taught in the home. Because of the fact that teenagers, Christians and nonbelievers alike, begin to solidify a personal world view by asking the question, "Who am I?" we implement its answer into the spiritual legacy we provide for our children. We must be prepared to help guide our children through the years when they discover the exciting truth of their true identity from the Lord's perspective.

Of course, teens have other questions, as well. When we begin to weave the threads of a child's spiritual legacy, we are wise if we prepare him for his turbulent teenage years by demonstrating answers to some of life's important questions:

Hope–Is there any hope for the survival of the human race with terrorism and nuclear war hanging over us? Why bother with trying to change anything? Nothing matters anyway if we are all going to be blown up.

Death–What if I'm scared to die? Is there life after death? What happens to me when I die?

Love–What is true love? Where can I find it?

Truth–Are there absolutes? Or can I just do what I think is right in my own heart and everything will be okay? Will I ever know the truth about the universe in which I live?

Values–What helps me to make moral choices in life? Why should I make choices to do what is right rather than doing what I want to do?

Suffering–Why is there suffering if God is good?

Evil–What can I do about the evil in the world? There's

so much evil. What good does it do to try to fight it? Do both good and evil exist in the spirit world? How do I know there is a spirit world beyond the physical world?

To a great degree, the answers a teen gets to these questions will determine how he views his world. I cannot imagine why any parent would want to wait and let his child grapple silently with these questions as a teenager or a young adult. We must begin answering these questions through our own actions and attitudes. Then gradually, but consistently, we must help our children find the answers to these questions in the Word of God. And in training our children to have a Biblical world view when they are young, we will begin to rescue the next generation.

IN SUMMARY

Our first three objectives in training are grouped under the categories of spiritual objectives, emotional objectives and social objectives. These three form a three-fold cord spoken of in Ecclesiastes 4:12

These three also form the substructure in building a child's character, which is the foundation. The superstructure is the building itself and is discussed in Chapters 8 and 9.

The greatest blessing in a child's life is to give him a spiritual legacy through the actions and the attitudes of his parents.

If we fulfill our God-given responsibility as parents, then we will seek to establish a firm foundation in the life of our children by giving them a strong spiritual legacy. Giving a spiritual legacy does not happen overnight.

Three foundational truths in establishing a spiritual legacy are to hear from God, learn God's ways, and maintain a pure conscience.

A pure conscience is maintained by confessing and forsaking sin, making restitution if necessary, and asking for forgiveness.

It is never too late to begin giving your child a spiritual legacy.

An essential component of a spiritual legacy is helping the child to establish a world view from a Scriptural perspective rather than from a secular one.

Chapter Six

Objectives in Training
SECTION 2: Emotional Legacy

The first thread of the three-fold cord which we need to impart to our children is a spiritual legacy, which will fortify the other two threads, the emotional and a social legacies. Likewise, the spiritual thread is strengthened by being entwined with the other two. One of the keys to training our children to live as godly Christians in a corrupt world and to impact it with their lives is to understand the goals of an emotional legacy and how it works.

Objectives of an Emotional Legacy

One of the questions I hear often from parents is, "How can I give a strong emotional legacy when I was not given one?" This is a good question, and I have a good answer for it. Even if a parent did not receive a strong emotional legacy, he can still give one to his children. As a matter of fact, churches are filled with people from all walks of life who struggle with painful childhood memories or crippling emotional experiences. These childhood experiences follow them into adult life and can even affect them as parents. However, a parent can determine to reverse the effects of the negative experiences of his youth.

One thing I do to encourage parents who have come from negative influences is simply remind them to have faith and believe that God can use even those bad experiences to help them raise their children differently. For example, if a parent had a father who used his tongue to

> *If their basic needs are not met or they feel threatened, children can sustain injuries that will affect them throughout their adult lives.*

criticize and censure, this younger parent can remember that and use his tongue to applaud and acclaim. We can take the negatives and turn them into positives for our children. This is not to say that there will not be moments when we fail, perhaps in the same manner as our parents. But we do not have to stay in that failure; we can rise up, confess the failure, and begin anew. Establishing a strong emotional foundation for our children is to be the goal. We must keep our eyes focused on that rather than on the one failure.

How do we go about establishing strong emotional foundations for our children? How do we give them an enduring sense of security and emotional stability? How do we provide an environment for our children that will assure them that they are safe and loved? We begin by considering how our children "tick" and what their needs are.

As seen in the chart below, Abraham Maslow developed what he called a hierarchy of the needs of all human beings. He said that only when the lowest need is met are people ready to move upward.[1]

Self-actualization

Self-esteem

To be loved or to belong

Protection and safety

Basic needs of food and water

Naturally the basic needs of food and water are in the foundational position in Maslow's chart because if they are not met, a child will obviously be incapable of receiving the others. When the basic needs for sustenance are met in a child, he will then search for protection and safety. When this need is met, he will seek to be loved by parents and to belong within a family. Only after he feels loved is a child able to develop a healthy self-esteem, and upon this foundation a child can achieve what Maslow termed "self-actualization." When he reaches this point, he is then able to enrich his own life, help others and move toward maturity.

Most of our children are raised in an environment in which their basic needs for such things as food, water, protection and safety are provided. Some of them, but not all, feel that they are loved and that they belong within the family unit. If their basic needs are not met or they feel threatened, children can sustain injuries that will affect them throughout their adult lives. Furthermore, a parent who fails to meet these needs in his children violates his God-given responsibilities and is guilty of abuse, an issue I will discuss later.

Although it may seem rather obvious, the first thing parents must recognize is that it is they who give the sense of security and unfailing love to their children. Others may contribute in this, but first and foremost, it is the parents who will build a strong emotional foundation for their children. I will assume that all parents realize the necessity of basic sustenance, then, and move on to the next essential in providing an emotional legacy for our children.

Protection and Safety

The approach we take to providing protection and safety for our children will vary according to their ages. While a parent will naturally hold his toddler's hand as he crosses the street, this would be frowned upon by his seventeen-year-old son, and most of us are aware of the ways in which we would physically protect our children. Nevertheless, perhaps we should start with the very basic element of protection.

The number-one area to consider is the need to protect our children in the spiritual realm. While I do not intend, at this time, to fully deal with the matter of spiritual warfare, it is clearly taught in the Bible that we do not "wrestle against flesh and blood, but against principalities, against powers, against the rulers of the darkness of this world, against spiritual wickedness in high places."[2] This battle for our children and for their minds is very real, and we deceive ourselves if we think that the Devil does not have weapons of destruction aimed at our children. As he seeks to devour and to destroy them, it is our spiritual protection of them that keeps him from achieving his evil intent.

We provide this protection first through prayer. We do it through coming before the Father's throne and petitioning Him to guard our children against the plans of the Enemy. We must ask Him to reveal any weapons that the Devil has formed against our children, and then we must listen and be ready to hear God's still, small voice speak to our hearts and reveal the Enemy's plan to destroy our children. After we have listened to God, it is very important that we speak. We must speak aloud the written promises of God over our children and set them forth as declarations of God's protection. Then we must watch. We must watch for any attempt of the Enemy to enter in and steal away that which belongs to God. Our next step is to fast. On the behalf of our children, fasting should be a habitual thing in our lives. And as we fast, we must again pray. We must fast and seek God's protection over our child. We must pray that God's purposes be fulfilled in the lives of our children and that the Lord will defeat all the plans of the Enemy.

It takes time and consistency to build a strong emotional foundation beneath our children just as it takes time and consistency to erect a building.

We must not stop at the bottom rung on the ladder of our children's need by supplying them with food and water. We must stand in our God-given authority as parents and protect our children spiritually. We must pray for them as we drive to work, as we wash the dishes, as we fold the clothes. We can listen to God regarding their lives as we go to the mailbox. Instead of watching television, we must watch their lives. And we must fast for them before they do not need us to fast for them rather than waiting, as is our common tendency, until we are in the middle of a crisis to fast. We should pray and fast on a continual basis. Then, when we are faced with a crisis, we will have the power of the Lord upon us because our continual prayer and fasting will have prepared us for such a crisis. In case I have failed to be clear with regard to this issue, let me repeat myself: It is our responsibility as parents to take this matter seriously and protect our children in the spiritual realm.

One thing that we need to understand before we go any further in examining the objectives of an emotional legacy is that it takes time and consistency to build a strong emotional foundation for our children. It will happen gradually and over a period of years, not days. Construction engineers recognize that it takes time and consistency to erect a building. They have to dig down into the earth before a building can be seen above the earth. They do not dig a hole one day and begin construction the next day because they recognize how important it is to build a firm foundation before attempting to construct any portion of the building. They also realize that consistency is a key to accomplishing their task. A building would never be erected if the engineers worked for several days and then forgot about their project for several weeks. Unfortunately, more than anything else, consistency seems to be a stumbling block with parents as they raise their children. Once a parent has committed to consistency, he can begin to build the atmosphere in which his child can develop and mature in emotional safety.

To be Loved and to Belong

As parents, we must ask ourselves, "What is the surrounding influence in my home? What is the main effect that the atmosphere in my home has on people? Is it friendly, or is there constant chaos? Is there more shouting than calm speaking? Is harshness prevalent instead of kindness?" If we do not like the answers to these questions, we must set about to change them. The atmosphere in our homes will directly influence the emotional stability of our children, and in order to be secure and emotionally stable, they must know that they are loved and that they belong.

First, love is what nourishes a child's spirit regardless of his age. Even teenagers who have never had the sense of being loved respond to an atmosphere of love in time. Psychologists tell us that it takes at least six weeks to change any given habit; therefore, if our homes have not had the atmosphere of love, we must give it time to change. We must go before the Lord and ask Him to help us to establish homes built on love and then allow Him time to work. And we can have faith in God's promise that "love never fails." This will take consistency, but the benefits to our children will be worth the effort because it is our emotional stability that gives us the ability to cope with all of the harshness, disappointments and trauma that life often introduces to us.

To be loved and to belong are two separate elements, yet they are two sides of one coin. If our children are loved, then they will have the sense that they belong to something. In being identified as a part of a loving family, they will experience a sense of belonging. However, it is important that parents carefully involve each child in family activities and seek to express love to their children openly.

When I speak of love, I do not mean the material love given by parents in the '50s. In many ways, it was easier for those parents to buy material things for their children than to take the time to mold their characters. However, the indulgent "love" given by parents in the '70s is not the love our children need either. Those parents, who were products of the "me" generation, appeased their children in the same sense that they were seeking to indulge and excuse themselves for being so self-centered. We must practice a balance in our love for our children, and this balanced love includes discipline. The sad thing is that often the expression of love from parents to their children just "comes out the wrong way." Discipline is not to be done in fits of anger or out of some concern that a parent's authority is being abused. With this type of discipline, a child can easily be mistreated. If we love them, the Bible teaches we will discipline our children for the purpose of correcting their character.

Love is what nourishes the spirit of a child regardless of his age.

Along with being very attentive to our methods of discipline, one of the things parents must be really careful about is giving of themselves. One of the constant complaints that I hear from teenagers in my travels is that parents simply do not listen to what they are saying. We love our children, yet we will sit in front of a television neglecting to listen to them when they try to get our attention. When they finally do get our attention, we often hear their words but do not really hear what they are saying because our minds are still occupied with the television program. One of our biggest failures as parents is that we do not listen with our hearts. We must listen with our full attention. There is a real need for us to listen to all of the information being given to us from our children. We love our children, but it is much easier to go buy them a new pair of tennis shoes or their own computer, for example, than to spend time training them about the different types of music and why some music would do them harm rather than good.

Of course we all love our children, but sometimes we have to contemplate the meaning of love a little more carefully in order to express it properly. Along with giving ourselves to our children, we must take them, as well. Love means recognizing that all of our children are quite different in many ways. Loving and fulfilling a boy's needs as a sturdy little choleric (quick tempered) may be quite different from ministering to a little girl's bubbly, sanguine (cheerful temperament) personality. Giving them each unconditional love means recognizing their differences. God formed each of us in the womb and orchestrated every small detail about our characters and personalities, and He did this on purpose. As parents, we must study our children and seek to determine why the Lord formed each child as He did. We should prayerfully seek God about each child and ask His purpose for that child's life instead of trying to shape him into whatever we want him to be. We are not given the privilege of raising children for the purpose of living our lives over again through their lives. It is our job, instead, to direct our children onto the path of God's purpose. Loving a child means knowing who he is as an individual and helping him fulfill the destiny that God has for him. Few things can fill a child with a sense of being loved and belonging more than knowing that he has been individually created by Almighty God for a purpose. And this security comes from loving parents who actively love their children as individuals.

Unconditional Love

Most of us have heard the term "unconditional love" and how important it is, yet we still struggle with giving this type of love. One of the first steps we take toward establishing a healthy emotional foundation for our children is to give them unconditional love throughout their lives. This unconditional love stems from the heart of God. It means accepting ourselves and accepting others, regardless of actions. If we take our example of love from the heart of the Father, we will balance it with a conditional recognition of behavior. This means that no matter what our children do, we will love them, but it also means that we love them too much to let them do whatever they want. There are times when a child's behavior and attitude must be disciplined. Unconditional love and a conditional recognition of behavior are like the two railroad tracks upon which a train travels. If one is not there in a parent's love, the train will crash.

Because of the cultural self-centeredness under which most parents were themselves raised, many are incapable of unconditional love. Although a parent's love comes the closest to unconditional love, most find it difficult to love without establishing conditions. We like to think that we love our children unconditionally, but more often than not, our children perceive our actions toward them as saying, "I will love you if..." However, one of the keys to developing unconditional love is the recognition that failure is a part of all of our lives. If our children fail, they fail, and this should not change our attitude as parents toward them. We should follow the pattern of God's unconditional love, which does not change no matter how often we fail. If we fail to make it clear to our children that we love them even when they fail, they will feel guilt and anger that can paralyze them in their emotional stability.

Unconditional love means that we love our children no matter what they do, yet we love them too much to let them do whatever they want to do.

It is our love for our children that will help them, when they fall, to stand to their feet again, brush themselves off and continue to walk through life. It is through our love for them that we teach them to accept the fact that their humanness will cause them to fail. And it is the strength of our unconditional love for them that will help them to rise up and move on. Our unconditional love is also the greatest picture of the Father's love for them. If they have been loved unconditionally by their parents, they will find it easy to perceive the love of the Heavenly Father when they are adults. When they fail as adults, they can then go into their emotional computer and see that

they are still loved in spite of their failure. It is this knowl-edge that helps them to get up and go forward. On the other hand, if they do not have the security of this unconditional love, they may give up after a setback or a failure.

In I John 4:15-21, unconditional love is expressed in this way:

> Whosoever shall confess that Jesus is the Son of God, God dwelleth in him, and he in God. And we have known and believed the love that God hath to us. God is love; and he that dwelleth in love dwelleth in God, and God in him. Herein is our love made perfect, that we may have boldness in the day of judgment: because as he is, so are we in this world. There is no fear in love; but perfect love casteth out fear: because fear hath torment. He that feareth is not made perfect in love. We love him, because he first loved us. If a man says, I love God, and hateth his brother, he is a liar: for he that loveth not his brother whom he hath seen, how can he love God whom he hath not seen? And this commandment have we from him, That he who loveth God love his brother also.

However, many parents do not realize how often we send a silent message to our children that says, "If I love you, this is how you must respond." As I mentioned before, along with giving themselves to their children, parents must take their children as they are, notwith-standing discipline. And accepting our children for the persons whom they are is a part of unconditional love.

A sanguine mother might not demonstrate the same

type of unconditional love to a child with a melancholy nature, who prefers to sit in an empty room and read a book, as she would to a child who prefers to be surrounded by a bunch of laughing people. Conditional love does not allow for the unique personality of each child to develop. Conversely, loving our children unconditionally means loving them exactly the way they are right now and not the way we think they could be or should be. Loving our children is recognizing the differences in personalities and characters.

Understanding different personality traits may require that we stop watching the television and go find some books on different personality types and learn how to deal with them in our individual children. Loving our children unconditionally is saying, "You are wonderful exactly as God made you to be. Even if I don't fully understand how you can like reading a book rather than choosing to go to the zoo the way I would have at your age, I still love you."

It is the strength of our unconditional love for our children that helps them to rise up and go on when they have failed. And it is the greatest picture of their Heavenly Father's love for them.

Being a parent who gives unconditional love also requires encouraging our children instead of berating and condemning. We need to allow our children to grow, for they need to develop in their own timing and in accordance with their individual personalities. Also, remembering our personal failures when we were our children's ages helps us to understand

when our children fail. We feel their struggles because we have struggled. As parents, we need to learn the difference between "fixing" and giving loving support. We often try to go in and "fix" our children's problems rather than giving them the loving support they need to fix their own problems. A positive support system is what will enable our children to grow wings and fly.

Another mistake that many parents make is placing their children on a performance track. The child of these parents receives this message: "I love you and I accept you if you perform to my expectations." For years I have publicly and privately said that all children are not capable of getting an "A" on a report card. A child may do his very best and work as hard as any other child in the church or in the family but be incapable of giving their parents an "A" on their report card. We parents need to realize that the best that a child can do is what should be honored and noted. Another problem with parents who expect A's is that they do not give their children any room to bless them because they already expect the best. In other words, to a parent who expects an A, and for a child who brings home an A, the child cannot bring home anything that Mom and Dad are not already expecting. Parents need to allow their children to surprise them, and they need to express pleasure when one of their children goes above and beyond what he has done in the past. If we neglect to do this, we risk causing our children to become performance-based individuals, conveying the message that they are acceptable only as long as they perform.

I have chosen to emphasize the need for unconditional love so strongly because it seems to be especially lacking in this generation that fulfills Paul's words to Timothy about those in the end times who will be "lovers of self." I do not mean to suggest that we should not discipline our children. Of course, it is essential that we keep our love balanced by setting up boundaries for our children, and this will be discussed in Chapter 10. Also, I have not dealt with the top two steps on Maslow's hierarchy of needs, as there are numerous Christian books dedicated to these needs.

My emphasis has been on the elements in the middle of the hierarchy, protection and safety and love and belonging. These two elements are essential to the physical as well as emotional well being of our children. Our children are vulnerable. They seek protection and love from us as parents, and they naturally seek approval from us, as well. Furthermore, regardless of what our response is to them, they accept our actions as being legitimate and true even when these actions are, in truth, abusive.

Emotional Abuses

Emotional abuse is often not recognized by either parents or children. If we emotionally abuse our children, it usually begins when they are young. Since children have no way of knowing that abuse is wrong behavior, they usually simply accept it. Sadly enough, some parents do not recognize it either because they were raised with it, themselves. We may have accepted the lifestyles that prevailed in our parents' homes as normal and then brought those same lifestyles into our homes. It is a miserable truth that we sometimes do not realize the long-term effects of our actions upon our children emotionally.

Long after the sting of a spanking has worn off, the memory of cruel words live on in a child's mind—often for a lifetime. I remember a young sixteen-year-old girl at camp who told me that her mother had become very angry with her when she was just seven years old. This incident between mother and daughter had taken place nine years prior to our conversation, yet the young girl was still struggling to believe that God would love her. When kids wonder if God loves them, it is often because they have not experienced love from their parents and it is difficult for them to receive love from a God they have never seen. During the incident in the life of the young girl mentioned above, the young girl's mother put her finger just inches from the end of the seven-year-old child's nose and said in a fit of anger, "I'm going to ask God to forgive me for the day I ever gave birth to you!" Those words burned into the heart and memory of that little girl. She went on to tell me, "You know my mother may have forgotten that day or the words she said to me, but I can tell you that I remember it clearly." We need to remember that a spanking is often forgotten more quickly than cruel words. They are difficult to eradicate. As parents, we must be careful what we say to our children.

Emotional abuse also occurs when we minimize our children's feelings or imply that our children are immoral or wrong for feeling a particular way. For example, a child's anger may be rejected or frowned upon by parents who believe that anger is a sin. If a child is not allowed to appropriately express anger, it will be pushed back and held in to seethe and turn into bitterness. One of the most common abuses in this arena occurs when a father will not allow his young son to cry because he was taught by his father that it is a sign of weakness. It is repulsive to the father that he may have a son who is weak and so he emotionally abuses his son by denying

§

him the right to cry. Unwittingly, this father is teaching his son that he should not have these emotions, so the cycle continues. The son learns to deny such feelings and then teaches his son the same.

Emotional abuse also takes place when children hear their parents say things like:

> "You aren't good at math. Nobody in our family is good at math."

> "You're just like your Dad's side of the family. They were all stupid."

> "You're so clumsy. You'll never make the basketball team."

These are fairly direct forms of abuse, but there are other unspoken messages that sink deep into the hearts of children. This type of abuse happens when parents compare one child to another:

> "Everyone knows that Sally is the prettiest girl in the family."

> "Johnny always was smarter than his younger brother."

> "Emily sings like an angel, but I swear Mary Jane sounds like a bullfrog."

Even if parents are joking lightly or mean no harm in what they are saying, children take these comparisons as condemnations that say: "You're not good enough. They are, but you're not."

There are times when parents are abusive to their children

through the way they communicate with them. When parents do not listen to their children, it builds up walls of frustration within the children. It shouts to them, "You're not worth our attention. We have much more important things in our lives than you." And children are also harmed emotionally if their parents continually ignore ideas that come from the children. In a sense, this is intellectual abuse. It communicates, "You never have any good ideas." And sometimes parents actually communicate intellectual abuse to their children by calling them stupid or dumb. The ramifications of these abuses can be devastating to children. Few children who are abused in this way develop into self-confident adults. They do not believe in their innate abilities. Most of them do not even like themselves as adults. They grow up insecure and feel that their ideas are never worth sharing or mentioning.

Identity Abuse

Another type of abuse happens when parents try to live their lives through the lives of their children, as I mentioned earlier. Sometimes parents push for their unfulfilled dreams, goals, and desires through their children. Generally, these parents have failed to reach their own goals, so they force them into the lives of their children. Many of these children grow up feeling that they never had their own childhoods. They are forced into molds formed by parents rather than being encouraged to pursue the destinies that God has chosen for them.

Still, other children get criticized because they don't match their parents' expectations. Either the children yield under the pressure to conform to what their parents want for them, or they rebel and suffer the rejection of the parents. This is because parents so often measure their own sense of self-worth by what their children do or how their children appear to other people. Parents often fail to consider who their children really are because they do not seek to find what God's destiny is for their children. This abuses a child's identity because he cannot see himself apart from what his parents wants him to do or to be.

Sexual Abuse

It almost seems extreme to mention sexual abuse in a book that is addressed to Christians. However, there is an element of safety for our children that must be addressed. This precaution is applicable to all children; girls as well as boys. There is an astonishing number of adults who were sexually abused as children because their parents did not use wisdom in providing a net of protection around them. Certainly, we assume that this was due to ignorance on the part of the parents, but the sexual abuse of our children has become so prevalent that this issue must be addressed. It is our responsibility to protect our children from all kinds of abuse. If we are protecting our children spiritually and are praying continually about and for them, then the Lord will reveal any plot by the Enemy to harm them.

Nevertheless, parents must exercise discernment when it comes to this matter. Mothers and fathers must exercise grave discernment regarding with whom they allow their children to be alone. Statistics sadly reveal that it is almost always someone within the family who is guilty of abusing our children. How can our children feel safe if someone within their own families violates them? If our children are to be given a strong emotional foundation, then they must feel safe and protected, and it is our responsibility to provide this environment of safety and security. Also, this protection of our children does not stop when they become teenagers. It is naiveté on the parents' part to be unaware of who their children's friends are and know nothing about their friends' families. This is especially important when our children get old enough to go out in cars with their friends. Parents still have the responsibility to protect them, and the first step in that protection is knowing who their friends are and what their families are like.

Sexual abuse is seriously grave because it involves more than emotional abuse. It is a combination of physical, emotional, and identity abuse. Sexual abuse has a debilitating effect upon a child and his ability to mature into an emotionally strong adult. As parents, we must be willing to do whatever it takes to protect our children from this insidious type of abuse.

The sexual abuse of our children has become so prevalent that we can no longer ignore the possibility of its coming into our midst.

We need to strive to build a strong emotional legacy for our children, and commitment to a good emotional foundation assures that we will give protection and safety to our children. It assures that we will take seriously our responsibility to protect them from the harm the Enemy has devised for them and that we will raise them in an environment of love and with a sense of belonging to a family.

IN SUMMARY

Our churches are filled with people who struggle with painful childhood memories or crippling emotional experiences, but we can reverse these emotional patterns for our children.

There are certain basic needs of food and water, as well as protection and safety, that we need to provide for our children in order to begin the process of building a strong emotional foundation beneath their characters.

One of the primary ways to protect our children is by doing it in the spiritual realm through prayer, listening, speaking, watching, fasting and then praying some more.

The Lord has given us the responsibility of protecting our children, and we need to stand in our authority as parents because of the plans of the Enemy regarding our children.

It takes time and consistency to build a strong emotional foundation for our children.

Unconditional love for our children means that no matter what they do, we will love them, yet it also means that we love them too much to let them do whatever they want.

The strength of our unconditional love for our children is what helps them to rise up and continue on with life when they fail.

We need to guard against our children suffering emotion, intellectual, identity or sexual abuse.

Chapter Seven

Objectives in Training
SECTION 3: Social Legacy

The final thread in the three-fold cord can sometimes be considered somewhat insignificant. However, like the other two, it is a part of one strong cord which provides a tether for our children and helps to keep them moored while in an unstable society. Also, the social legacy completes the substructure which we seek to build into the characters of our children. If we adhere to the objectives regarding the spiritual, emotional and social legacies, then we will have laid a firm foundation, a solid substructure, for our children's lives. Combined with the strands of a spiritual and an emotional legacy, the social legacy is vitally important because it deals with teaching our children about relationships.

Objectives of a Social Legacy

So what is a social legacy? The dictionary gives several definitions to the word "social," but they can mostly be summed up in two words, "people relationships." If we are to fully equip our children to enter into the adult world, then we must endow them with the skills to interact with other people. Unless a child flees to a desolate cabin where he endures the reclusive, withdrawn, unsociable existence of a hermit in some remote hideaway, he will be interacting with people for the remainder of his life. It is our responsibility to equip our children with social refinements, and this includes much more than proper table manners and knowing how to introduce someone properly, although these matters of etiquette are part of the social legacy.

The importance of relationships is established in the Bible. When the Pharisees, Sadducees and lawyers questioned Jesus on what the greatest commandment was in the law, He replied that the first was to love God and the second was to love our neighbor as ourselves. Coupled with the commandment to love the Lord, Jesus spoke of the importance of our relationships with one another as being the essence of the entire law. Then, the apostle John further emphasized the significance of relationships when he said, 'We know that we have passed from death unto life, because *we love the brethren* (italics added)."[2]

Setting the boundaries in a child's relationships is best done by his parents, and the best classroom for teaching people skills is the home. Within the secure environment of the home, children can learn the critical lessons about respect, responsibility, love and courtesy to other people. Proper relationships need to be taught in two broad areas, those within our home and those without the home. Dealing with people might be one of the largest hurdles in life that our children learn to jump. If we succeed in teaching our children how to relate well to others, then we have taught them a vital element in the task of living.

Even as the spiritual and emotional legacies which we outlined above are essential, so is the social legacy in building the substructure of our children's characters. If we want to see our children become responsible adults, then we must prepare them to interact with other people. The Golden Rule, "Do unto others as you would have them do unto you," is perhaps the hallmark of social responsibility. Contained within the meaning of Jesus' words is the element of respect.

Coupled with the commandment to love the Lord, Jesus spoke of the importance of our relationship with one another as being the essence of the entire law.

Respect

When Jesus said that we should love our neighbors as ourselves, He allowed for the assumption that it is out of a reservoir of love for ourselves that we can love others. This does not refer to a self-centered, selfish kind of love, but rather a love and respect for one's self that stems from knowing he is a child of the Lord. Without this respect for ourselves, we have no reservoir from which to respect others. If we do not respect our own possessions, then we will not respect the possessions of others. If I

do not respect my own achievements, then I certainly cannot respect the achievements or abilities of others.

Teaching children to respect others should ideally be done at a young age, but it can be accomplished at any age. We must remember, however, that the fruits of such a change may not be evident for several weeks, and instruction must be cushioned in love and consistency.

Our children need to be taught a healthy self-respect as early as possible, and we begin creating this self-respect within them by being role models for them to imitate. Children first learn to respect themselves by learning to honor the worth of parents who walk in virtue before them. The Bible clearly teaches to "honor your father and mother," and there are no exceptions to this commandment. Honor comes with the position of being a parent, as the commandment clearly states. However, we parents are also responsible for being worthy of this honor, or respect, from our children. If a child witnesses his father continually criticizing and maligning his mother, it becomes difficult for the child to respect his father. The child may never voice his disrespect to his father openly, yet two things could occur as a result of this father's example: The stature of the father may diminish in the child's eye or he may ultimately follow the pattern of his father. Likewise, if a mother speaks disrespectfully about her children's father, then how can they be expected to learn respect from her? If parents do not treat each other or their children with respect and if children only have disrespect paraded before them, then it is impossible for children to learn to respect others. On the other hand, if children observe a mutual respect between their parents, they begin to absorb it. These parental actions that show mutual respect and self-respect become silent standards for children.

In addition to respecting each other, parents should respect their children as individuals. As parents, we often fall into the habit of clustering all of our children into one pigeonhole, and we lose sight of their uniqueness as individuals. Yet, they are individual creations of the Lord, each unique and special with their personalities, talents, gifts and abilities. Cultivating these individual traits says to our children, "As unique, individual human beings, you are worthy of respect."

Perhaps the language that is best understood by children regarding respect is the language of possessions, both their own and those of others. I have known adults who have total disregard for others' possessions. They will borrow something, carelessly allow it to be broken or damaged, and then return it in defective condition without volunteering to replace or repair it. A close look into the homes of these individuals often reveals the same type of disregard for their own possessions. Gifts that were given to them are tossed into the corner and covered with cobwebs. Clothes are piled high and go weeks without laundering.

We are the role models who teach our children how to have self-respect and respect for others.

This disregard for possessions shows a lack of respect for that which hard work and effort has worked to earn. I am in no way stating that our possessions should be placed before us as idols of materialism and greed, yet

God has given us a principle for managing that which He has placed in our hands. Christ instructed the disciples to gather up all that remained of the fish and loaves that God had miraculously supplied because He respected that provision. This principle goes all the way back to the Garden of Eden when God told Adam to keep and dress the garden. That which we put hard work and effort into demands respect; it is not to be treated as an object of idolatry, but it is to be respected.

We live in a disposable society. Things are no longer repaired; they are replaced. This mentality has infected the thinking of our teenagers, which is precisely why they have such disrespect for possessions. Many of them have never had to pay anything for their possessions. All of their needs, wants and pleasures are provided for or supplied. Very few young people know what it is like to really have to work to own something, or to maintain something or even to purchase something that is not quite perfect and then have to work to repair it to bring it up to its standard. This is why so few young people have the proper respect for possessions.

Respect for possessions is not a natural human trait. If our children are not taught to respect possessions, then they will be careless not only with their own possessions but also with the possessions of others. Furthermore, lack of respect for possessions builds up the negative character trait of wastefulness, and the Lord never blesses that. This unsavory trait will follow an untrained child throughout his life. His home will reflect this disrespect and will generally be unorganized and chaotic. This disrespect for possessions will also follow him into the workplace, where it could have unfortunate repercussions with employers or fellow employees. As human beings, we are all territorial, and part of that territorial instinct involves our possessions, including things that we perceive to be our possessions. Although a stapler may in reality belong to the company, if it sets on the desk of the accountant, then in that accountant's mind it is "his stapler." If someone walks into the accountant's office and takes "his possession," this can often be the first shot fired on Fort Sumpter and easily lead into a civil war within an office. These are not imagined situations that will face our children in the grown-up world of business. It behooves us to prepare them with the proper respect for possessions.

A mother came to me once complaining that her oldest child, a teenaged son, had absolutely no regard for the possessions of his younger brother and sisters. I suggested a formula for teaching him this valuable lesson. First, the mother went home and issued a warning to her son as I had suggested. The next time he misused one of his siblings possessions, she would reciprocate with something of his own. He nodded his head and walked away. Three days later, the teenager's younger brother complained to the mother that his favorite t-shirt had been ripped during basketball practice while being worn, without permission, by her oldest son. When the mother confronted her son, he mumbled, "Oh yeah, I told him I was sorry." The mother said nothing. Rather, she walked to her son's dresser and picked up a brand new bottle of his favorite, very expensive, cologne. Her son had just purchased the cologne with his last paycheck from McDonald's, where he worked part time. The mother opened the new package, walked to his bathroom, and proceeded to pour the contents of the bottle down the drain while her son screamed in protest.

She then demanded enough money from her son to replace the younger son's t-shirt. The next time I saw her, she had a glowing face and a good report. To this day, her son respects the possessions of other family members. If our children respect their possessions and the possessions of others, they are on their way to successfully crossing the bridge that carries them from childhood into adulthood.

Responsibility

Like unconditional love and conditional recognition of behavior which I mentioned earlier, respect and responsibility run side by side like railroad tracks. Respect encourages responsibility. If we succeed in teaching our children to respect their own possessions and the possessions of others, then we also teach them responsibility. In learning to respect possessions, they learn to take on the responsibility of caring for their own possessions, as well as the possessions of others.

Some children are more naturally inclined to be responsible than others. Young Don was the oldest son in his family. His father was an alcoholic who hanged himself in jail. His mother was a rather simple, country person who never grasped the truth of how essential it is for children to have responsibility modeled for them by their parents. Consciously seeking to develop character in a child lay beyond her abilities. Don could have steeped himself in self-pity over the shame of his father and the inadequacies of his mother, but he had a sense of responsibility. When he was twelve years old, he worked as a caddy on the golf course and brought the majority of his money home to help support his mother and younger brother and sister. Don never had the role model of a responsible parent, yet he determined to take the road of responsibility rather than complaining about the platter that life had placed upon the table before him. Although Don made the right choice and taught himself responsibility, it is generally something that is learned by our children rather than chosen. Parents cannot assume that their children will teach themselves as Don did, and they must regard the individual strengths of their children as they teach them.

Feelings of Others

One of our objectives in giving our children a social legacy is to teach them to be sensitive to the feelings of others. Just as they must learn to respect others possessions they must learn to respect others feelings. This is part of the boundaries that we set for our children in the area of social training.

It is often said that "children can be so cruel." In a sense, this is very true. Children often inflict wounds on each other that are deeper and longer lasting, than any harsh reprimand of an adult. For example, a soft spoken, shy child from Romania suffered one day at the hands of some school children in an almost inhumane way. Because the girl could not speak fluent English, the children gathered around her one day after school and began to taunt her mercilessly. The poor child had no defense, and no other child came to her rescue. She walked off the school grounds and headed toward her home. By this time, a crowd of at least fifteen to twenty children surrounded her on either side and followed behind her shouting derisive insults at her the entire time. They continued to follow her for several blocks. Overwhelming fear and glaring humiliation must have clutched at the young girl's heart as she trudged home in the midst of such a taunting crowd.

Any parent seeking to equip his child with a social legacy will ask himself, "What would my child have done if he had been present at that scene? Would he have been part of the crowd? Would he have bravely come to the defense of the young girl? Would he have laughed? Cried? Become indignant? Gotten angry? How would he have responded in such a situation?" And a parent would naturally also wonder about something else: "Suppose that had been my child. How would he have responded to such treatment?"

We can give our children a strong spiritual legacy, but if we do not develop them socially, then we will have failed in building a truly firm foundation for them. It takes all three; the spiritual, emotional and social legacies, to build a superstructure beneath the characters of our children. And just as the spiritual and the emotional objectives outlined above are taught in the home, so are the values of respect, responsibility and sensitivity to others' feelings. We must teach our children that people are important. Furthermore, our children need to learn to be responsible and respectful as they interact with different people.

Common Courtesy and Communication

Courtesy to one another is another petal on the flower of sensitivity to others' feelings. One mother raised her children with this adage: "If you can't be kind to your family members, then don't waste your manners on those outside the family." Kindness and courtesy should be extended to every family member, every day, in every situation. Consistent courtesy is what we should aim for in our family relationships, and if we do, a habit of courtesy will naturally overflow into our relationships outside the home. If respect and courtesy are the transcending rules of our homes, then these traits will be what our children learn. Moreover, that which is begun with a toddler will follow him into his teen years. Former President George Bush stated in one of his speeches that he would like us to return to a "gentler" time. This was not an old man reminiscing about the "good old days" and one who was not in touch with the realities of this generation. It was a desire to return to the gracious habit of simply being courteous to each other as human beings. This character trait seems to have been passed on to his son, President George W. Bush. Common courtesy has been lost over the past two decades, yet it is a necessary component of our children's social inheritance.

We can give our children a strong spiritual legacy, but if we do not develop socially, we will have failed in building a truly firm foundation for them.

All relationships, of necessity, produce some form of communication. Even the Lord's relationship with us has a goal of communication. Since the boundaries established in the social legacy we desire to give our children involve communication with them, all of our communications should be cushioned in our unconditional love for them and acceptance of them as individuals who are worthy of respect as human beings. And naturally, we should be careful to exhibit the same courtesy within our families as we do with others like our pastors,

teachers, co-workers and fellow students.

One of the biggest complaints of teenagers is that there is no true communication between them and their parents, a problem which generally begins when they are small children. It is only after they enter into their teen years and begin to struggle with the mixture of the child and the emerging adult within them that they begin to voice their discontent. However, if our children are raised in an environment that celebrates their uniqueness as individuals and we listen, really listen, to them when they are young, then this problem will be lessened when they enter their teen years. The communication between parent and child must be protected and respected. If we want our communication with our children to remain open through their teen years, then we must lay the foundation of listening, learning, growing and enjoying a lively exchange of ideas with our children from the time they are small.

Social Graces

Along with common courtesy, social graces are an important part of the legacy we provide for our children. Social graces can be defined as "polite behaviors in public relationships with others," and children who are strengthened in the social graces are commonly considerate of others, are apt to be self-assured, and have the confidence in handling themselves in a variety of social settings. If we teach the simple social graces to our children, then our well-mannered children will grow into self-controlled adults who will find that polite behavior can prove to be a real benefit when looking for a job, dealing with difficult people or attending a church with a multitude of personalities. Social graces are practical and sensible, and they are a practical extension of the Golden Rule. They are for the whole family, and the more our children know about good manners or social graces, the better they will feel about themselves and about others.

Before you dismiss this section as inconsequential, listen to this story. For years a certain grandmother sought to teach her granddaughters proper manners in order to prepare them for the adult world. The father of her grandchildren, however, ridiculed her efforts and said such things were not necessary. Out of partial embarrassment because they were not taught at a younger age by their parents, the granddaughters modeled themselves after their father. The grandmother pleaded her case, insisting that if they never had any need for proper table manners or other social graces, then there would be no harm done, but if the time ever came when manners and social graces were needed, then her granddaughters would be prepared. Her pleas were drowned in the Christian father's laughter, which was followed by her granddaughters' jeering and claiming that they did not care. However, the day came when the oldest granddaughter desperately wanted to marry a young man who was preparing to be a doctor. He was cultural, gracious, spiritually mature and well-schooled in social graces. After the first date, the young granddaughter pleaded with her grandmother to give her a crash course in manners, but it was too late. The granddaughter could not learn overnight what should have been assimilated over the years. The young man went elsewhere to find a Christian wife who would not be an embarrassment to him.

Was it unfair of the young man to choose another lady? No. He had the good providence of being raised by parents who were by no means wealthy but who realized the need to teach their son social graces. He simply wanted to find a wife with the same social legacy. And good manners and social graces are more than knowing which fork to use at the dinner table. Having good manners involves having the right attitude toward ourselves and toward others, something the young lady mentioned above lacked. The point here is that skill with social graces can influence many things from respect for elders to future relationships.

Teaching our children some basic social graces is essential to the health of their self-esteem. Most children will not return home after a social event and tell their parents that they felt self-conscious or embarrassed because they did not know which fork to use or how to properly introduce someone, yet this happens to children all the time. Feeling comfortable with good manners helps our children to have respect for themselves, and without this confidence in knowing how to behave in a social situation, they will feel awkward, self-conscious, inferior and embarrassed. Do we want our children to feel this way? Of course not.

The dictionary says that manners are "socially correct behavior." They are simply a matter of how we behave toward one another. If we teach our children good manners, then we are teaching them how to show respect and consideration for others. Manners, correctly taught, are not simply a veneer that we put on, but they come from the heart. Good manners are really a form of love as shown in the Bible:

> Love is patient, love is kind. It does not envy, it
> does not boast, it is not proud. It is not rude, it is

not selfish, it is not easily angered, it keeps no record of wrongs."[3]

There are plenty of books on the market that can help us to teach our children manners at any age.[3] Also available are light, easy-to-read, heavily illustrated books that will help teenagers feel more comfortable with social graces.[4]

The best option, however, is to daily instill these social graces into our children within the environment of the home, where we can motivate them with godly love. We can allow our children to practice using the right fork at our dinner tables rather than suffering the embarrassment of choosing the wrong fork at some banquet when they are teens and so susceptible to the approval of their peers. Our children can practice introducing people properly with us rather than having to shrink back in a public situation. Telephone manners, writing thank-you notes, personal manners, restaurant manners, guest manners, and a whole list of others can all be taught within the protection of our private homes. We think it is a cute thing when a small 5-year-old child answers the telephone, speaks properly, asks the correct questions and then quietly goes to get his mother or father, but this should not be considered out of the ordinary. All of our children should be given this social legacy of knowing how to respond properly in relationships both within the family and outside the family.

IN SUMMARY

The importance of the social legacy is that it deals with our relationships with each other.

The Lord stressed the importance of relationships when He stated that next to loving God, we need to love our neighbors as ourselves.

As in the other two foundations which we seek to build beneath our children's characters, that which the parents demonstrate before the children will overpower anything that they could speak to their children.

We need to develop self-respect in the characters of our children, as well as respect for other people. Teaching the proper care for a child's personal possessions and for the possessions of other people is often the channel for teaching respect.

Respect and responsibility are like two railroad tracks running side by side. Without one or the other, character will crash like a train on a faulty railroad track.

Teaching children to be sensitive to other people's feelings is part of setting the boundaries in the social legacy.

Common courtesy and communication are vital components to building a firm foundation in our children's social structure.

Social graces and manners are polite behaviors in our relationships with other people and should be instilled in children at a young age. However, it is never too late to teach our children.

Chapter Eight

Objectives in Training
SECTION 4: Physical Legacy

The three objectives in the last chapter can be viewed as being the inside or the hidden aspects of our children's training. Remember, the spiritual, emotional, and social legacies are comparable to the substructure that is hidden beneath the ground, yet they are prerequisite to providing a firm foundation for the superstructure. For our purposes, the superstructure is the physical and moral legacy we want to give to our children. The physical legacy is, perhaps, the most noticeable in the lives of our children, as they inherit various physical traits, which compare with the varied buildings which are constructed above the ground. The more important superstructural aspect we impart to our offspring is a moral legacy. The moral legacy that is offered to our children by the world is corroded. If we are to save this generation, we must set about re-establishing the moral foundations of our nation one child at a time.

This may appear to be an impossible task, but it is not. It is God's method. He places a tiny speck of a grain of sand upon the shore in order to form a beach. That beach, composed of nothing more than a combination of tiny grains of sand, holds back the mighty force of the ocean so that it stays within its bounds. Forming character into our individual children has the same potential power of holding back the forces of darkness. We must not lose heart. This can be done, and we can begin to see the results of our training within the era of our children's generation.

Objectives of a Physical Legacy

The bodies of our children are absolute masterpieces of the Creator. They are miracles. No computer can ever hope to compete with the human brain. No pump is capable of matching the intricate power of the human heart. And no camera or lens can ever equal the human eye as it was designed by God. Our children's bodies, as well as our own, are truly works of art by the Lord. David recognized this when he said, "I am fearfully and wonderfully made."[1] We are all "designer originals" because God carefully fashioned us as individuals.

From birth, we ought to teach our children to recognize the gift of their physical bodies. If we have substantiated the substructure of a spiritual, emotional, and social legacy for our children, then we must recognize that God put the right body around the right spirit in our children. If we are to show gratitude to the Lord for His superlative gift of life, then we should teach our children to treat their bodies with dignity and respect. It is our responsibility to teach them how to care for their bodies.

We Are What We Eat

What we put into our bodies is important; it is true that we are what we eat, and if we feed our bodies healthy food, we will have healthy bodies. Initially children are totally more dependent upon their parents for the type, of food they are fed. Unfortunately, there are many parents who are "hooked" on junk food, and they feed their children the same. There is a popular saying among those who work on computers: "Garbage in, garbage out." This bit of wisdom is applicable to our bodies, as well.

It is our responsibility to guide our children in eating balanced meals. Although the middle-aged years of our children are rarely considered, what we teach regarding their diets today can affect them in their later years. Physicians tell us that many prevalent diseases such as heart disease, diabetes, gastroesophageal reflux and even musculoskeletal problems that attack our bodies today are partially a result of bad eating habits. Therefore, the eating habits we teach our children can actually become a matter of life or death to them when they are older. There has also been an alarming increase of weight gain among our

If we are to save this generation, we must re-establish the moral foundations of our nation, and we will do this one child at a time.

135

children. Obviously, extra weight and bad eating habits can follow them into their adult years and harm them physically.

Equally important with a balanced diet is a good exercise routine. Years ago, it would have been unnecessary to stress any type of exercise for children because children normally crawl, walk, run, jump, leap and play enough to exhaust most adults. Statistics prove, however, that we have raised a "couchpotato" generation that spends much more time sitting in front of televisions and computers than running and playing outdoors. Because of this, our children have suffered. As parents, we can provide numerous opportunities for our children to get physical exercise. We may choose to involve them in team sports or individualized programs. Some families enjoy camping, hiking or doing simple daily yard work together. Even a simple walk together in the evening can provide valuable exercise and family fellowship. Leaving a healthy physical legacy to our children will justify our efforts in the health and longevity of our children, and it is a part of our responsibility as parents.

Personal Hygiene

Our grandmothers used to tell us all the time, "Cleanliness is next to godliness," and many of us grew up thinking that was a commandment in the Bible. The saying is not found in the Bible, but there is great value in physical cleanliness. While it was something that the '60s generation almost lost sight of as they determined to turn their backs on all that society acknowledged, the purpose for teaching children personal hygiene is fairly fundamental. Laying this foundation of good personal hygiene for our children in their early years gradually teaches them to respect and to care for their bodies as the temples of God. If we seize these opportune moments to emphasize caring for God's temple when our children are young and seek our approval and attention, we capitalize on the ideal time for teaching them the wonder of their bodies. These little lessons also cultivate the communication between us and our children regarding their bodies and how special they are in God's mind.

It is a wise parent who lays a foundation early for the adolescent years when a child's body begins to demand its own voice in sexual matters that barrage him daily in music, entertainment, television, movies and other media. One important aspect of this foundation is to daily demonstrate the significance God places on our children's bodies in these small matters even as the Lord instructed the Israelites to "teach them diligently unto thy children, and shalt talk of them when thou sittest in thine house, and when thou walkest by the way, and when thou liest down, and when thou risest up."[2] The key to teaching this principle is that it is begun early and done on a continual and daily basis, not just when some crisis suddenly raises its head in the home. Also, if there has been a concentrated effort to lay the substructures of spiritual, emotional and social foundations, then moving into this physical area is most natural. These lessons of daily life revolving around physical matters when our children are young have a greater purpose that will surface when they reach the turbulent teen years and their bodies are clamoring to be acknowledged.

Sexual Purity

Where does one begin in trying to paint the picture of

the monster that has sunken its claws into the very heart of our nation's children and teenagers? The illustration that I used earlier regarding Christian teenagers who think it is okay to perform oral sex because there is no penetration is real. It is happening all across our nation, as it has just recently happened in the White House. Even the former president of the United States told the American people that he did not have any sexual relations with some woman because it only involved oral sex! In William Bennett's latest book, *The Death of Outrage*, he comments on President Clinton's impropriety: "Sex is the most intimate of all human acts; it is fraught with mystery, passion, vulnerability . . . sex is a quintessentially moral activity, and they [societies] cannot therefore be completely indifferent toward it."[3] Self-deceived and disgraceful role models in such high positions give credibility to the excuses teenagers offer in justification of their own actions. Furthermore, our children have been so brainwashed through the popular music, entertainment, television and media that they know nothing other than what the world teaches them about sexual purity. In *When Hollywood Says Yes, How Can America Say No?* Gene Wolfenbarger gives compelling evidence and statistics of the sexual immorality that is promoted among Hollywood and television filmmakers:

> Research studies give approximations about what the average person views regarding sex: 9,230 sex acts, or implied sex acts, a year on television. Of that sexual activity, 81 percent is outside the commitment of marriage. This means that the average young person, watching ten years of television from age eight to eighteen, watched 93,000

scenes of suggested sexual intercourse, and 72,900 of those scenes would have been pre- or extramarital. What kind of impression does that make on young people...[4]

There is assuredly a cultural war going on in America and our children are the spoils. We cannot afford to ignore this raging battle. We must guard and protect those little specks of sand that the Lord has placed in our care and do our best to build that substructure of a spiritual, an emotional, and a social legacy into the lives of our children. For some of us, that means getting on the front line and taking the arrows from the Enemy. For some, it means staying on our faces before the Lord and interceding for God to intervene on behalf of our children.

Let me share a few of the statistics from *When Hollywood Says Yes, How Can America Say No?* I hope these statistics have a sobering affect upon you. I include them, for the sake of our children, to challenge you to do something about turning the tide in this drenching flood of sexual immorality. Please keep in mind that these statistics are almost a decade old at the time of the writing of this book. It is horrible to think how they may have escalated since they were gathered. Also, there is no single source that can be blamed for the following statistics. They are partial consequences of the '60s sexual revolution, Hollywood, music, movies, television, entertainment, and other media, all of which have played a significant role in establishing this cultural mind set that promotes sexual immorality. The breakdown of the family unit also has a part in contributing to our children's early involvement in sex and the sad, destructive consequences of sex which are charted below:

Information on Student Activity[5]

Two-thirds of America's 11 million teenage boys say they have had sex with a girl . . . By the time they are 18, on the average, boys have had sex with five girls.

Most boys had their first sexual experience at age 14 and girls at age 15.

Of those students who have gone through a comprehensive sex education program, 65 percent are sexually active, a percentage almost twice as high as those who have not completed a sex education curriculum.

According to the Sex Information Education Council of the U. S. (SIECUS), one out of every two boys and one out of every three girls between the age of 15 and 17 have had sexual intercourse.

Wolfenbarger goes on to mention a survey that was conducted by the Rhode Island Rape Crisis Center which "revealed some rather shocking results."[6]

In different schools across the state, over 1,700 students between the sixth and ninth grade attended adolescent assault awareness classes. The students were asked if a man had the right to force a woman to have sexual intercourse with her if he had spent money on her. The results of that survey are shocking.

Nearly 25 percent of the boys and 16 percent of the girls said yes! Then 65 percent of the boys and 47 percent of the girls in seventh through ninth grade said it is okay for a man to force a woman to have sex with him if they have dated for six months or longer. And 51 percent of

140

the boys and 41 percent of the girls said a man has a right to force a woman to kiss him if he spent a lot of money on her "which was defined by twelve-year-old children as $10 to $15."[7]

Information on Teen Pregnancy[8]

The United States has the highest incidence of teenage motherhood of any Western country in the world.

Each year, 1 million adolescent girls become pregnant. Of those who give birth, half are not yet 18 years of age.

The birth rate for unmarried teens rose an additional 14 percent from 1980 to 1985, following an increase of 18 percent during the 1970s.

Partially resulting from this imbalanced logic are the following unnerving statistics on teen pregnancy:

Teenage motherhood among school students is so prevalent that a Dallas high school established a 15-bed nursery for students with children and Houston dedicated two entire high schools for the same purpose.

The scope of this book is too limited to continue to record the myriad statistics that are available regarding the physical consequences that sex has had upon our young people, but they are devastating. Pornography has become a billion-dollar business in America: "Last year Americans spent more than $8 billion on hard-core videos, peep shows, live sex acts, adult cable programming, sexual devices, computer porn and sex magazines."[9] Sexually transmitted diseases have reached the epidemic level in our society with AIDS being our nation's number-one health menace. Wolfenbarger also gives us this sobering information: "It is estimated that 1 to 1.5 million Americans are currently infected with the virus . . . It will probably prove to be the plague of the millennium. 'If you were the Devil,' says Dr. Alvin Friedman-Kier, AIDS researcher at New York University, 'you couldn't conceive of a disease that would be more disruptive and disturbing than this one, a sexually transmitted disease that kills within a short period and for which there is no treatment.'"[10]

Sexually Transmitted Diseases[11]

Sexually transmitted diseases are no longer reserved for prostitutes or wayward GIs in foreign countries. They are infecting people from all economic and social strata at the rate of 33,000 people a day in the U.S. alone.

That means 12 million cases a year, up from 4 million in 1980. At this rate, one in four Americans between ages fifteen and fifty-five eventually will acquire an STD.

Anyone who has sex outside of marriage is at risk. STDs do not recognize a person's religious or moral beliefs, only his or her actions. As one researcher said, "Unless you're monogamous for a lifetime, with a monogamous partner, you're at risk. And the more partners you have, the greater the risk."

The Minnesota Institute of Public Health warns that "there are twenty sexually transmitted diseases which are not prevented by contraception." They emphasize that fifteen million people now get a sexual disease each year.

Dr. Edward Weismeir, director of the UCLA Student Health Center, warns students that, "Even an honest answer to an intimate question is no guarantee that a person is safe. While dormant in one person, an STD can be transmitted to another." He admonishes then that "one chance encounter can infect a person with as many as five different diseases."

Until recent years, public health experts counted barely five types of sexually transmitted diseases. Now, they know that more than twenty-seven exist. Research shows that the number one concern of women–ahead of even war "and peace" –is sexually transmitted infection.

Physicians and researchers offer very little hope for those who have contracted AIDS and limited means of prevention regarding other STDs; however, some of America's known experts have begun to point their fingers back toward morality and monogamous relationships in an attempt to ward off this seemingly insurmountable problem of sexual promiscuity that has possessed our nation:

Causing the most concern is AIDS

One of the biggest lies that our culture has accepted is the one that proclaims the "fun and freedom" of sexual immorality. The romance and defense of sexual freedom are always promoted as being glamorous and appealing, and the intrigue of sex is always elevated by the entertainment industry. The flip side of the romance coin, which is broken and shattered lives, is rarely revealed. From the time our children are young, they are bombarded with sexual innuendos from their cartoons up

143

until the time they are promoted into the endless cycle of soap opera stars climbing in and out of numerous beds with various partners. Even the Walt Disney company, that anchor of children's entertainment, has recently harmonized with the rest of Hollywood. This legendary company now creates its female characters as sensual adults, and going beyond that, the artists prostituted and perverted their talent by drawing the male sex organ in a castle on the cover of the "Little Mermaid" video.

The consequences of the sexual revolution of the '60s are staggering, and our children are the true victims. They have been raised in a culture that has had its moral fiber ripped asunder. And yet–and yet, there is hope. We can turn things around. For the sake of our children and our grandchildren, we must reverse the order of our culture.

IN SUMMARY

The physical bodies of our children are unique and specially created by God to be holy temples for His habitation.

The physical and moral legacies that we impart to our children are the superstructure in the building of their character.

We are what we eat.

The practice of personal hygiene with our children does more than keep them clean. It affords opportunities to teach them God's perspective on the truth that they are "fearfully and wonderfully made."

Sex is the most intimate of all human acts and should be taught from the Lord's perspective and not that of the world. Forbidden sex vs. sexual purity is a decisive battle in the cultural war that is currently being waged in America.

The statistics are unnerving regarding sexual activity among our young people, and its consequences continue to mount in their intensity.

Chapter Nine

Objectives in Training
SECTION 5: Moral Legacy

There is such a crossover between the objectives of the five legacies I have outlined that it is sometimes difficult to make a clear-cut separation. For instance, one of the primary objectives in giving a good, healthy physical legacy to our children is to promote in them sexual purity, which is a moral issue. While there is a definite crossover between these legacies and their objectives, there is also a distinction.

Objectives of a Moral Legacy

The word "moral" has almost lost the vigor of its meaning because the media has made reference to it in such disparaging contexts that we are almost apologetic when we reference the word, except when we are within the safety of Christendom. Yet it is a good word, and its meaning is realized in the Bible. God based His dealings with Israel on the moral context of the Ten Commandments, and declaring the Ten Commandments and the teachings of Jesus to be foundational, our founding fathers went about the task of constructing a government that found its strength in the morality of its citizens. They wisely formed our nation to be governed by those who adhere to a standard of right behavior. The problem, even as our forefathers speculated from the beginning, arises when the citizens of America lose the operation of conscience or ethical judgment. Our Constitution was formed with the understanding that ethical, moral individuals would be the country's leaders in both government and society.

The dictionary defines "moral" as "teaching a conception of right behavior; conforming to a standard of right behavior; sanctioned by or operative on one's conscience or ethical judgment." The problem in this first decade of a new millennium is that we have a wrong conception of right behavior. Our culture has held up a perverse moral standard and we have conformed to that standard as right behavior. Finally, then, our national conscience and ethical judgment have been grievously damaged.

Realizing this confusion regarding morality helps us to understand why we find ourselves in the current moral dilemma. This is why a president of the United States of America can stand before the American people and flagrantly lie. This is why a president can carry on an illicit affair with someone young enough to be his daughter and feel justified by his definition of what constitutes sex. America's conscience has been seared. From the White House down to the street person, we as a people have had our national conscience destroyed. We lack the understanding of how profoundly God, merciful and kind though He may be, opposes a nation which calls good evil and evil good. The current situation in our nation reflects how deeply entrenched immorality has become within our country. And this is all because our concept of morality has become weak and anemic.

Even as good physical health usually dictates a strong posture, there is also such a thing as a strong moral posture. While sex is often an identifying landmark to reveal the posture of an individual or a nation, morality encompasses more than sex. In giving a moral legacy to our children, we make a big difference in our children's world view; in how they interpret and interact with their world.

We have had our national conscience destroyed in America. We call good evil and evil good.

One of the most important aspect of moral legacy involves the things we allow our children to view and therefore ponder. With regard to the physical legacy, I stressed the importance of being clean on the outside, but it is just as important to be clean on the inside. Do we know how our children look at the moral standards taught in the Bible? Have our children secured these standards on the inside, or do they merely quote to us what they know we want to hear? How do they look at the presidential scandal that has occurred in our country in the last decade?

Think back over the past month of your child's life. How often did you sit down and personally read to him from the Bible, discuss issues from the Bible, or witness his reading the Bible himself? Often? Rarely?

Now think back over the amount of time that your child watched television, listened to the radio or the stereo, went to a movie, listened to the news media, sat before a computer or read a magazine. Most of us will have to confess that our children spend much more time under the above-mentioned influences than they do in the Word of God. What values system do you suppose your children are absorbing? It is certainly not that of the Bible. Our children are digesting, bite by bite, the world's philosophy of moral standards.

In this section, I will focus on the influences of visual entertainment, music and media industries that mold and shape our children's concept of morality, as well as the formal education of our children as they sit under the daily influence of their teachers. Unless we as parents recognize the inherent power within these industries and systems, we ignorantly offer our children to be sacrificed.

Sacrificing Our Children to Devils

A very educated, fashionable woman recently approached me after church. I knew some of the background of her life, and listened as she discussed her young teenaged daughter at length with me. The daughter was multi-talented, extremely intelligent and quite attractive. Snapshots of the young teenager verified all that the mother told me. The pictures were shots of the young lady, from age 11 and on into her teens, in heavy make-up and low-cut dresses. It grieved me as I looked through the stack of pictures to see such a display of the attempt to turn the innocence of a lovely young child into the premature look of a model with such heavy make-up. As the pictures revealed each stage of the maturing young lady, her dresses became shorter, tighter, and lower. I thought about how the Lord is not a prude, but He has set certain standards for dress. One of these standards is modesty, a principle mocked by today's culture.

This mother had taken our culture's standards for her daughter, rather than adhering to those set by the Lord. She had entered her daughter into every beauty contest, dance contest, and talent contest in their part of the country. During the course of our conversation, it became quite evident that she was reliving her life through her daughter. Bragging on her daughter's intelligence, beauty, talents and abilities illuminated this mother's face. Yet, when she walked away, I heard a still small voice within me say, "They sacrificed their sons and daughters to devils."[1]

Are our children getting their values system from the Bible or from the entertainment, movie, television and music industries in America?

Hearing that rather strong statement so startled me, that I went immediately to my Bible to locate the verse and read its context. I discovered a very sobering passage of Scripture. The verse that I heard spoken to my spirit is found in Psalm 106, which outlines the story of Israel's rebellion against God and His continual mercies toward them:

"But [they] were mingled among the heathen, and learned their works. And they served their idols: which were a snare unto them, Yea, they sacrificed their sons and their daughters unto devils, and shed innocent blood, even the blood of their sons and of their daughters, whom they sacrificed unto the idols of Canaan: and the land was polluted with blood. Thus were they defiled with their own works, and went a whoring with their own inventions. Therefore was the wrath of the Lord kindled against His people, insomuch that He abhorred His own inheritance."[2]

When I read this passage, I shuddered inwardly, realizing it as the Holy Spirit's estimation of this situation. Yet, this

Our children live in a chaotic culture that has no values system other than one that is bent on the destroying their innocence and devouring their purity.

mother who so vigorously pushed her daughter onto the stage of the world's system of achievement would have been vehement to think that she could be guilty of sacrificing her child to devils.

In my heart, I truly believed that the mother was ignorant of what she was doing. At the same time, however, the words became crystal clear and took on an application of admonition that I had never applied to our generation before that moment. The parents of today are literally sacrificing their children to devils and do not realize what they are doing. How can this be? One of the reasons that such a thing is possible in our day is that we insist on seeing the image of an altar with an animal tied upon it when we think of sacrifice. Yet there is another definition for the term "sacrifice," which suggests that we suffer the loss of something or the destruction or surrender of something for the sake of something else. What I am saying here is that today's parents willingly participate in the destruction or surrender of their children, although such participation may be done in ignorance, for the sake of being prosperous, popular, successful and fashionable by the standards of the world rather than the standards of God. In this way, today's parents are sacrificing their children to devils.

Stating that parents are sacrificing their children to devils may seem to be harsh and unfair; and it is bone chilling, but it is not meant to be accusatory. Rather, this statement is intended to be a window through which we can see the true nature of our Enemy. Through this window we may also get a glimpse of his strategy as he seeks to destroy our children through the cultural influences in America that have already been instrumental in ripping the moral character of our nation to shreds.

Again, I recognize the role that the breakdown of the family and education have played in the immorality that prevails in our nation today. However, I specifically want to ferret out the monumental destruction that has taken place in the characters of our children because of the cultural chaos that stems from the various entertainment industries. If we knowingly allow our children to absorb the world view of these influences, then the blood of our children stains our hands. As God's Word exhorts:

> When a righteous man doth turn from his right-
> eousness, and commit iniquity, and I lay a stum-
> blingblock before him, he shall die: because

thou hast not given him warning, he shall die in his sin, and his righteousness which he hath done shall not be remembered; but his blood will I require at thine hand. Nevertheless, if thou warn the righteous man, that the righteous sin not, and he doth not sin, he shall surely live, because he is warned; also thou hast delivered thy soul.[3]

The inventions of radio, movies, television, records and the computer are testimonies to man's ingenuity, and, in themselves, they are not sinful. They are simply instruments. It is the use of these instruments that brings about the damaging effect in our culture, as they can be used for either good or bad. Unfortunately, the majority of the entertainment industry has shifted toward uses which are harmful for our children. Although Hollywood loudly protests against the accusation that it is doing anything wrong, the evidence is undeniable. Let's look at these different factors that so influence the thinking and the attitude of our young people today. It is not difficult to see how warped the values system of our children has become because of these scourging influences.

The Morals of Hollywood and the Television Industries

As John MacArthur aptly notes, there is "no sin more destructive to the conscience than the sin that takes place in the arena of the mind."[4] For the first time in man's history, the Devil has more access than any other system or individual has to the minds and morals of our children, through the media of Hollywood, television and the music industry. And the professional entertainers in these industries have a completely different view of morality than God's people do.

For decades now these industries have produced the slandering propaganda that has devastated the morals of our society at large. However, if confronted on the immoral content of their "art" and its effect on our children, the leaders of these industries instantly hide behind the excuse that they are mere entertainers who have no philosophies or agendas to promote. This simply is not true, because there is always an "element of conscious or unconscious value judgment"[5] hidden in every decision to produce a movie, a television show, or a popular song.

Hollywood has taken the last vestiges of human dignity and paraded them on panoramic screens in order to shock and arouse audiences. Nothing of a private nature has been left undone in the movie theaters. Nude bodies writhing upon each other have become a common scene in the majority of movies. Masturbation and oral sex have been viewed in technicolor on wide screens by millions. Mockery and laughter regarding private body parts are frequent. The popular scene of someone on the toilet on the big screen now has a competitor, going into the bathroom at big events to watch some actor urinate. Also popular are scenes of someone spewing forth vomit even when such scenes

The devil has more access to the minds and morals of our children through the medium of Hollywood and television than any other means known to man.

serve no purpose within the story. And these nauseating, graphic scenes of vomiting are what Hollywood simply refers to as "the portrayal of realism." All of this is considered "art," and Hollywood loudly protests its constitutional rights if someone dares to complain about such vulgarity. Furthermore the more vulgar, coarse and crude the perversities are in the films, the more Hollywood hails them as works of art.

More insidious than Hollywood's blatant perversity are the subliminal messages employed by the film and television industries, and they have been cemented into the soul of American life. Sex? Why not? Everyone does it. Because our children are raised in a society that has polluted our minds, our souls and our spirits, they understand clearly that Hollywood's standards have become our standards. Openly promiscuous scenes of nudity, sex, and perversion are praised by filmmakers with no thought of the consequence upon our children who are raped of their innocence if they are allowed to view such scenes.

For decades now, movie and television producers have scoffed at and ridiculed those who stand for the basic Judaeo-Christian morals upon which this nation was founded. "The Last Temptation of Christ" spearheaded the campaign of Hollywood in its attempt to affront the religious sensibilities of most Americans. Since Mary Magdalene appeared on screen with her body tattooed from head to toe, Hollywood has flagrantly shown a determined effort to mock things of the Lord. And no religious denomination is exempt. In the movies, those who profess the Lord in any respect are almost always the deranged, demented fools in the cast of characters. These subliminal messages that mock morality have successfully worked their way into the minds of

156

America's citizens.

In being filled with graphic and illicit sexual scenes which insult and ridicule things of the Lord, movie and television programs have produced a new morality for America. After decades of viewing these "standards" set by Hollywood and television, what else can we expect our children to do but embrace this value system of shameless sexuality and scoffing of the sacred. And there is still more.

Those who actively fight the sexual content produced by Hollywood also oppose another element that is prevalent in movies. . . violence, which is just as rampant as sexual content. Although the producers and filmmakers in Hollywood argue against it, "decades of violent entertainment have succeeded in altering the public's perceptions and values" to the extent that our society has become desensitized to the violent content in movies and television.[6] However, the influence of these violent images is seeping out through such things as the multiplying incidents of teenage violence in drive-by shootings and senseless killings of friends in school cafeterias and classrooms. In *Hollywood Vs. America,* Michael Medved wrote:

Those who try to justify the industry's current excesses [violence] by pointing to long-ago releases that once shocked moviegoers are actually undermining their own case. The fact that movies formerly viewed as horrifying are now considered almost laughably tame, in no way demonstrates the innocuous or inconsequential impact of cinematic gore; if anything, it argues for the opposite conclusion, providing that decades of violent entertainment have succeeded in altering the public's perceptions and values.

Only the most jaded nihilist could take comfort from a situation in which bloody scenes deemed unbearably disturbing by past generations are now accepted as an integral element of the popular culture. This higher level of tolerance for media violence may even promote acceptance of the blood-curdling cruelty we experience with increasing frequency in our own homes and communities. It is hardly a positive development for a society when it loses its ability to feel shock."[7]

Medved continues by stating: "More than three thousand research projects and scientific studies between 1960 and 1992 have confirmed the connection between a steady diet of violent entertainment and aggressive and antisocial behavior."[8] While Hollywood continues to turn a deaf ear to these claims, there is overwhelming evidence that violence adversely affects our children. In 1982 there were volumes of social science surveys published regarding violence and its effect on our children and "the Surgeon General of the United States concluded that 'there is a clear consensus among most researchers that television violence leads to aggressive behavior.' Or, as following a five-year task-force investigation: 'The conclusion drawn on the basis of twenty-five years of research . . . is that viewing televised violence may lead to increases in aggressive attitudes, values, and behavior, particularly in children.'"[9]

> *"There is a clear consensus among researchers that television violence leads to aggressive behavior."*
> *–Surgeon General of the United States*

Year after year, evidence continues to pile up regarding the effect of violence on our children. There is both scientific and academic support for this conclusion. Are we to allow this violence to become a part of our children's moral legacy? Do you allow the graphic and illicit sex in movies and television to be viewed by your children? If so, this is the moral legacy you are choosing for your children. As parents, we cannot allow our children to view these sexually graphic scenes and violent images: If we do so, we sacrifice our children to Devils because these violent images and graphic scenes come from Devils, certainly not from the Lord.

We must constantly remind ourselves of the definition of the term "sacrifice": the destruction or surrender of something for the sake of something else. And we must quiz ourselves: "What am I willing to sacrifice my child for? Is it the convenience of allowing him to sit in front of a television set or attend a movie without first monitoring its contents? Is it ignorance of the damaging effect that sexually graphic material and bloody violence can have upon my child? Is it deprivation? The mother of whom I wrote earlier was not about to deprive her daughter of having fun and "succeeding" in life.

Finally, with regard to the influence of Hollywood upon our children, we must recognize that there is a decisive cultural battle being waged in our country. In spite of the astonishing evidence that is brought before Hollywood, its leaders and producers refuse to take responsibility. This is another reason that the moral legacy we provide for our children is so important. The following excerpt from Medved pertains to twenty-five leading academics and media researchers who gathered in Pittsburgh for a conference on "The Impact of the Media on Children

159

and the Family":

> Participants included distinguished faculty members from universities ranging from Yale to Northwestern, from Duke to Michigan State, from Rutgers to the University of Wisconsin, and they presented more than thirty papers and workshops in the course of the three-day program . . .one of the organizers of the conference, reported, "Given the diversity of participants, they reached a surprising consensus that values in much of the mass media, especially in violent and sexually explicit materials, are on a collision course with traditional family values and the protection of children."[10]

Sex, mockery of religion, violence. Is that the extent of this immoral monster that lurks around every corner seeking to devour the innocence of our children? There is yet another element that is claimed by Hollywood, television, and the music industry. Filthy language abounds not only in movies today, but it saturates the lyrics of today's popular music.

The Morals of the Music Industry

Another monster of immorality lurks around every corner seeking to devour the innocence of our children: words. Along with Hollywood and the television networks, today's popular music culture is infatuated with filthy language. While the film and television industries occupy themselves with the production of sex, urination, vomiting, maggots, butchery, slaughter and bloody violence, the music industry assaults the ears of its audiences with an almost obsessive fascination with foul language. Music groups today compete to produce the ugliest and nastiest language possible in their lyrics.

While we generally discourage our children from the use of such language, especially the vulgarities, if they listen to today's popular music they will be blasted away by overtly offensive language. And these verbal obscenities are not occasional. They fill many lines of today's popular music, especially that music targeted for young audiences. Foul language is used to express, for one thing, the sexual content of the music. Every sexual perversion imaginable, from incest to bestiality, has found its way into the lyrics of modern music. And if foul language or sexual perversion is not the theme of a song, then anti-religious sentiments are strummed out on the guitars of the rock 'n rollers or the gangsta rappers. Madonna, popularized by her irreverence to Christianity, was the beginning of a convoy of performers who tried to get attention by injecting religious elements into their acts. Another example is the heavy-metal group, Metallica, which sang about "The God That Failed":

Music groups that promote today's popular culture compete with each other to produce the ugliest and nastiest language possible in their lyrics.

> I see faith in your eyes, never you hear the discouraging lies
>
> The healing hand held back by the deepened nail, follow the God that failed.[11]

It was this irreverence toward religion and God that gave rise to the pentagrams and severed goat's heads on music album covers. In the past three decades, it has become increasingly popular among musicians to be devoted followers of the Prince of darkness. The music industry magazine, "Rolling Stone," wrote about one of the members of Kiss who leaped upon the stage and shouted out to the audience, "I find myself evil! I believe in the Devil as much as God!"[12]

Our Deeply Troubled Society

Hollywood, television, and the music industry love to excuse themselves from any blame when it comes to the problems within our culture. Instead, they claim that they are only faithful messengers who truthfully proclaim the bad news about the breakdown of our culture and the blood thirstiness of our society. Hollywood stubbornly insists that it does not:

Promote promiscuity

Justify sexual immorality

Tear down family values

Exalt anything ugly or base

Glorify indecency

Speak foul language

Display cruel humor

Mock religion

Recreate real-world brutality

Celebrate violence

Portray bizarre murders

Relish bodily mutilation

Yet the evidence is undeniable. Hollywood, television, and music are guilty of all of the above. And these transcending influences have literally changed the moral fiber of our nation. When we offer up our children to become victims of the out-of-control immorality that is perpetuated by these industries, then we sacrifice them to Devils. I have witnessed thousands of young people whose lives have been shattered because they have taken on the morality of these industries. I have looked into the blue eyes of a 16-year-old girl which should have reflected hope and innocence. Instead, they were glazed with hardness and promiscuity. I have listened to 11-year-old boys, whose conversation should revolve around football or soccer, as their coarse, filthy words focused on R-rated movies they had seen.

Are we sacrificing our children to Devils? The evidence within our society answers in the affirmative. This should alarm us! And it should cement our determination to be the deciding factor in changing our nation's culture. There are no shortcuts to restoring the foundations upon which this nation was built. It can only be done through the building up of character and the protection of that character one child at a time.

Almost all of us have heard or read the following words by Dorothy Nolte, but they bear repeating. They are a blueprint for us as parents:

> If a child lives with criticism, he learns to condemn.

> If a child lives with hostility, he learns to fight.

> If a child lives with ridicule, he learns to be shy.

If a child lives with shame, he learns to feel guilty.

If a child lives with tolerance, he learns to be patient.

If a child lives with encouragement, he learns confidence.

If a child lives with praise, he learns to appreciate.

If a child lives with fairness, he learns justice.

If a child lives with security, he learns to have faith.

If a child lives with approval, he learns to like himself.

If a child lives with acceptance and friendship, he learns to find love in the world.[13]

IN SUMMARY

The word "moral" has lost the integrity and vigor of its meaning, yet it is applauded in the principles in the Bible.

Our Constitution was formed with the understanding that ethical and moral individuals would be its leaders in both government and society and that without this base of morality, the government would not be effective. Giving our children a good moral legacy is foundational and should not be left to just "happen" on its own.

Mass media has a values system which will be absorbed by our children if we do not prayerfully protect them from it. And if we do not supervise and guard our children from these negative influences, we sacrifice them to Devils.

The moral fabric of our nation has been ripped to shreds through the overpowering influence of Hollywood, television, and music, and it is our responsibility to address this tragedy one child at a time.

PART III
PASSION WE MUST POSSESS

Chapter Ten

Realizing our Position
Section I

Malachi the prophet spoke of the time when Elijah would "turn the heart of the fathers to the children, and the heart of the children to their fathers."[1] This portion of Scripture is generally embraced by most scholars as being prophetic of the end times. Even a casual observation regarding our nation's condition today certainly confirms the need for the heart of the fathers to be turned back to the children and the heart of the children to their fathers. For America, turning the hearts of the children back to the fathers has a more far reaching implication than just the traditional family unit. America's children, from ages 1 to 100, need to have their hearts turned back to our founding fathers. History proves the truth that our founding fathers' hearts were turned toward us when they struggled to create our government.

The challenges that face all men, especially Christian men, are apparent to most of us. Whether we respond to them or not will depend upon our hearts, for it is the heart that turns the fathers back to their children. The foreseeable future for our nation does not appear very bright, but the stage is being set for brave men everywhere to walk to the center of their lives and their families' lives and assert their masculine leadership given to them by the Lord. As men, as fathers of the children in America, we must ask ourselves, do we realize the responsibility of *our* positions?

Earlier, I touched briefly upon mothers and their importance in the home. To underestimate the fact that the "hand that rocks the cradle, rules the world" would be foolish. The Lord has deposited a powerful tool called "influence" into the hands of all mothers. No one can deny the impact of any mother's influence upon her children. However, in this chapter I want to deal with the role of the father in the home and in our nation. While mothers were given the influence in the home, fathers were given the authority.[2] It is to the fathers that the ministry of Elijah is addressed. And the progression of the words of that prophecy is notable. The heart of the fathers is turned to their children first. Then the heart of the children will then be turned to the fathers.

While many a child would have been lost to the Devil if it had not been for the intervening prayers of his mother, I will emphasize the role of fathers at this point because of the importance God places on them. One important father in the scriptures is the father of the prodigal discussed in Part IV. It is notable that the Biblical story of the prodigal involved only the child and the father. Assuredly, there must have been a mother in the story, yet she is not mentioned. Also, the passage from Malachi mentioned above emphatically places certain responsibilities upon the shoulders of the fathers rather than mothers.

Realizing our Position

As fathers, we must realize the responsibility of our position. Fatherhood is a God-given position, and it bears a God-given responsibility of authority. Yet over the past three decades there has been a gradual trend among men, even Christian men, to occupy themselves with something other than the responsibility of fathering. Men have become passive dropouts as fathers, and regardless of the valor exhibited by women who try to fill in for fathers who do not realize their position, there is no substitute for the father and the authority invested in his position by the Lord. While there can be no denial regarding the mother's influence in the home, it is only the father who can give leadership and a sense of security to his children. And fatherhood involves priceless eternal influence and consequences. Until the fathers who sit on our church pews turn their hearts toward their children, there will be no effectual change in the lives of our children.

The Lord has deposited a powerful tool called influence into the hands of all mothers.

This turning of the heart is a personal work by the Holy Spirit in the lives of fathers. While the Promise Keepers movement among the Christian men in our country has been positive in its impact, the turning of a father's heart

171

toward his children still remains an individual work. Men can go to crusades and still not have hearts that are turned toward their children. Men can go to church and still have hardened hearts. When a father's heart is turned to his children, the determination and courage to make changes and to protect his children will follow.

Some time during the past three decades, men became passive and lazy in their positions as fathers. Without any doubt, it is easier to let women function in this position because the role comes with hard work. Somewhere along the way, men in general seemed to adopt the idea that if women want the responsibility and headache, they can have it: If women want control, they can have that, too.

Years ago, I heard a man make the remark that men had graciously surrendered in allowing the women's liberation movement to push them out of their male position. With good humor, he went on to say that if things had been reversed, the women would not have been so gracious. My question would be, "Why did you give up the position that God gave to you?" This is not an issue of men being gracious and women being ungracious or vice versa. It is a question of God's ways, which we spoke of earlier. It was God Who made the choice to give man the authority and woman the influence. To use again the example of the two railroad tracks, man's authority and woman's influence run perfectly

Many a child would have been lost to the devil had it not been for the intervening prayers of his mother.

side by side. When there is a crossing over into the other's territory, an inevitable crash occurs even if the one side willingly gives up its position. Even if men were gracious in giving up their positions, this does not negate the fact that God invested authority into the position of the male and the father and, graciously or not, men have abdicated that responsibility.

For three decades, beginning with the '60s, there has been a concentrated effort to blur the distinction between the sexes. The feminist movement may have been ushered in through the front door, but homosexuality, bisexuality, and unisex clothing came in the back door. Charles Swindoll writes about the blurring of sexual roles in his book *The Strong Family*:

> The separate distinction of male and female is not merely a 'traditional expectation'. . . And it isn't simply a 'role system that held industrial civilizations together.' It is a foundational block upon which any healthy civilization rests. When the roles get sufficiently blurred, confusion and chaos replace decency and order. When effeminate men begin to flood the landscape, God's longsuffering reaches the length of its tether, ushering in the severest judgment imaginable . . . a la Sodom and Gomorrah. Romans 1:24-27 is still in the Book, isn't it? Worse of all, because more and more men care less about being men, the family is thrown into confusion. Leadership is shifted to the wife and mother, and the children understandably reverse the roles, tragically perpetuating the unnatural trend.[3]

How is it that our fathers have forsaken their position as being fathers? Clearly they are influenced by the new culture that found its roots in the '60s revolution. And obviously the breakdown of the family unit has contributed to this. For decades now, our boys and young men have not had the proper role models either in the home or any other place in society. Fathers have fallen into the habit of providing "things" rather than their presence for their families. All of these facts contribute to the problem of a lack of masculine leadership. Most significantly, however, the American fathers of today were simply raised in the culture that had turned its back on all the traditional values systems held by those in the past.

I am not advocating that we return to the '50s when the father was the unrivaled head of the family with his Archie Bunker feet propped upon the bowed submission of his wife and children. Not at all. Nor am I advocating the selfish tyrant who lives in a fantasy world of his own importance. This matter goes beyond the '50s and right up to the throne room of the Heavenly Father. Men have been given the authority of their positions as a picture on earth of our Father in Heaven. We should tremble at such a comparison, yet this association should also set up the parameters of our fatherhood. We should look to Him and see how He sits in His position as Father to His children. And we must remember that this is a heart issue. The heart of the father must want to turn to his children.

Gentle and Unconditional Love

There are several outstanding characteristics lacking in fathers today, and one of these is unconditional love. Jesus' love eclipses every man's love because of His great sacrifice on the cross, yet His love is our example. And His love is characterized by gentleness; gentleness which forever altered the course of history. In the New Testament, Paul spoke of his apostleship as being one in which he was "gentle among you, even as a nurse cherisheth her children."[4] Some translations use the word "mother" here rather than "nurse." Paul uses this word to describe his manner toward them as his spiritual children. The idea is that the apostle's affection for his brethren is characterized by a gentleness normally associated with a mother. It is appropriate to expect a father to use this manner of gentleness with his own children.

A lack of gentleness among fathers today often blemishes their position. I have observed men in their interactions with their children, and after years of "father watching," I have come to the conclusion that most of them have not the faintest idea of how to be fathers. Regardless of a man's background, he is influenced by the pervasive concept that a father has to be manly and strong. To assert his own need to feel strong and in control, he is compelled to impart these "manly" qualities to his children, even if his child should happen to be a girl. Some of these qualities are good, but there is a time to impart them and there is a time to be gentle. It should go without saying that a father should especially exercise gentleness with babies and young children. This, however, is not always the case. More than once, I have seen weak and insecure fathers bounce and toss babies in a manner

How is it that our fathers have forsaken their position and their God-given authority to be the head of the house?

that is really not safe in an effort "to make them tough." Trying to make a baby or a one-year-old "tough" is hardly appropriate. The baby would probably rather have a clean diaper, and the one-year-old would rather his father toss him a ball rather than being tossed himself across the room onto a couch to instill toughness.

Often fathers do not seriously consider the magnitude of the fact that God has placed the character and life of a human being into their hands. They do not realize their position and the heavy responsibility that comes with it. Because they do not realize the weightiness of their position, they often resort to doing to their children what was done to them. Some fathers were forced into a role of tough manliness, so they unwittingly force their own children into the same mold. They desire to be good fathers, yet exactly how to do it eludes them. On the flip side, passive and insecure men simply look to someone else to carry the burden. Both types of fathers neglect to go before the Lord and seek His face for answers to the dilemma we face in both our families and our nation.

This is a heart issue. The heart of the father must want to turn to his children.

A Father's Exhortation

In writing to the church at Thessalonica, Paul compared his relationship with the Thessalonians to that of a nurse (clearly meaning "mother") who cherishes her children. He went on to compare the same relationship with that of a father and son. He wrote, "As ye know how we exhorted and comforted and charged everyone of you, as a father doth his children."[5] The three verbs Paul used here, exhort, comfort and charge, characterize fatherhood and should be our template. We should also note the progression of those words. As a father to spiritual children, Paul first exhorted, then comforted, and finally charged.

As fathers, our first objective, then, is exhortation. It has been said that a teacher aims for the head, but the exhorter aims for the heart. Since a teacher seeks to bring content of facts before someone for the purpose of their understanding, an exhorting teacher is the best of all. As fathers, we should all strive to be exhorting teachers. An exhorting father will gear his efforts toward edifying and encouraging his children rather than provoking them "to wrath."[6] The purpose behind a father's exhortations is to guide his children into a full, meaningful life, and one of his greatest joys will be in building the character of his children and helping them to reach their full potential.

I have observed the children of fathers who habitually exhort them. These children, who are given ample dosages of encouragement from their fathers, are almost always vibrant and positive young people. It is also much easier for them to find their roles in life than for those who have been denied exhortation. An exhorting father also helps his children to overcome their problems, not run from them. He builds his children up and strengthens them so they are capable of walking through problems, and he cheers them all the way. Then on the other side of their problems, he is standing at the finish applauding their victory.

Exhorting fathers have an extraordinary ability to take facts and teach their children how to walk them out in practical ways. They are masters at taking the facts in the Bible and teaching their children how to apply them in daily, practical living. These fathers take no chances when it comes to the application of important Bible principles in the lives of their children. They love to point out specific steps for their children to follow because they have already proven the direction of those steps by having walked through those steps themselves.

One exhorting father received a telephone call from his third-grade son's teacher. She was outraged that the young boy brought a frog in from recess and let it loose in the classroom. The incident had disrupted the entire class and for fifteen minutes there was complete pandemonium in the room. Throughout the entire conversation, the teacher repeatedly accused the father about "his son." Later when the father confronted his young son, he could not help but remember a similar incident from his own life as a child. Nevertheless, this exhorting father and son outlined three steps on paper for his young son. Together, they discussed each step. The father occasionally asked his son what he felt would be a more appropriate action than just mumbling a hasty apology. Father and son came up with these three steps of reparation:

> *Some fathers were forced into a role of tough manliness, so they unwittingly force their own children into the same mold.*

1. Apologize to the teacher for disrupting the class

178

2. Stay and help the teacher to straighten up the classroom

3. Volunteer to carry her heavy books to her car

The father received a telephone call the next afternoon from his son's third-grade teacher. She was exuberant with praise about the maturity of "her student" (not "his son") who had gone beyond her greatest expectations in apologizing. "Most children would not even think to apologize," the teacher said in glowing tones of enthusiasm and joy. "He not only helped me to straighten up the classroom, but he helped me carry some heavy books to the car. These were heavy books, too. He had to make two trips to get them all."

That night around the family dinner table, the son glowed from listening to his father praise him for the great job he had done with his apology. In the boy's trials, his father exhorted him to the right action and then edified him for having done so. The exhortation of this father taught his son that this failure in his young life was to be looked upon as an opportunity to produce personal growth rather than to produce shame.

An exhorting father is also fluent in his communication with his children. The first thing this entails is actually communicating or speaking to his children. This does not necessarily mean that a father has to have the skills of an orator. It does mean, however, that he has learned the art of true communication which is a two-way street. He not only speaks to his children, but he listens as well. Those people in the body of Christ who have the gift of exhortation, as mentioned in the scriptures, are examples of true communication. What they communicate is hope and encouragement, and an exhorting father will do the same in his communication with his children. He will keep his eyes focused on the solution rather than on the problems of his children.

I know of one exhorting father who has a marvelous ability to embrace his children as they are without judging them. He never sees the need to judge his children for where they are in their lives. Instead, he sees only their need to be helped so that they might take steps in the right direction. Three words are continually before him as he fathers his children and seeks to prepare them for adulthood: loving, forgiving, and accepting. He does all three well. On the other hand, a judgmental person emanates a silent condemnation. He may not even need to speak because his disapproval is apparent in his silence. Children may be forced to reside in the same house with such fathers, but they will close themselves off from them, and they will find it hard to receive anything from such a father.

Exhorting our children also means that we will "accentuate the positive and eliminate the negative." Fathers who do this know the secret of drawing their children with honey rather than vinegar. Their attitudes are generally always positive and they draw their children and others to them just by their optimism. They seem to say with their attitudes, "Got a problem? Great! What an opportunity for us to be overcomers in Christ Jesus!"

Exhorting fathers are those who not only communicate to their children verbally but they communicate through their lives. Deep within, they know that in order to have credibility with their children they must walk what they talk. Their faith and their values system is demonstrated daily before their children in practical ways. How blessed is a child who has an exhorting father who realizes the essential need to live the rhema Word of God, the living Word of God. A father like this not only believes in the logos, the written Word of God, but he understands that the rhema word must become flesh in him as he walks before his children. The exhorting father understands the reality of being able to teach only what he has appropriated within his own life.

Because of the trait of walking the walk and not just talking the talk, exhorting fathers cannot tolerate strained relationships. They tend to be immediate in trying to clear up any relationship problems. Often they initially take the blame in order to keep that relationship bridge built, even if they are not the one at fault. The foundation for this is true humility. Although a child might be the one at fault, the father seeks immediately to restore the relationship between himself and his child, securing the strength of the relationship before attempting a lesson on personal responsibility. And his example of quickly clearing up problems with others encourages his child to do likewise.

An exhorting father is fluent in his communication with his children. He has learned that true communication is a two-way street.

In addition to caring very much about personal relationships, exhorting fathers expect a great deal from themselves and from their children. It is as if these fathers have looked into the windows of their children's

lives and seen their children's untapped potential. These fathers have seen the abundant equipment that God has provided for his children, motivating them to reach higher until they can move into that potential. Fathers are likewise gifted with the ability to exhort their children to set higher goals for themselves and to reach them. Within every child is the desire to please both of his parents, but he especially needs to feel the approval of his father. I think this is based in the eternal truth of our seeking after the Heavenly Father. Children need the approval of their fathers, and if we exhort them in practical means of obtaining goals, then what a decisive and strong generation of children can we offer to the world!

At this point, I feel the need to stress something of utmost importance to fathers regarding this instinctive need of children to receive approval from them. There was a true saying that circulated years ago throughout the body of Christ regarding "strange women" (wayward women) and fathers. The gist of the saying was that it is fathers who are responsible for little girls turning into strange women. I might add that it is the Christian father who turns his little girl into a strange woman, not just the unbelieving father. Our little girls must receive the masculine approval they so desperately need. They must feel the safety and security of being loved by their daddies. This will eliminate their need to receive masculine approval by allowing boys the freedom to use their bodies.

The idea that fathers make strange women out of their little girls is pretty horrifying, isn't it? Perhaps it will remind us of the grave responsibility of fatherhood, our God-given position.

Finally, an exhorting father is characterized by "yes."

Charlie Shedd had it right when promised his son Peter that he would never say "No" if he could say "Yes:" In his book, *You Can Be a Great Parent*, he wrote:

> *Peter*, we see it often. Babies raised in a positive atmosphere develop much better personalities than those who constantly hear the words "No," "Stop," "Don't."

> Let me show you what I mean. This has to do with a dirty old bale of binder twine. When we moved from Nebraska to Oklahoma, we brought it along. I had used it there to tie sacks of feed and miscellaneous items. It cost something like $1.15. So I said *to your brother*, "Now, Philip, you see this binder twine? I want you to leave it alone." But it held a strange fascination for him and he began to use it any time he wanted. I would say, "Don't," "No," and, "You can't!" But all to no avail.

> That went on for six or eight months. Then one day I came home, tired. There was the garage, looking like a no man's land with binder twine across, back and forth, up and down. I had to cut my way through to get the car in. And was I provoked! I ground my teeth as I slashed at that binder twine. Suddenly, when I was halfway through the maze, a

Exhorting fathers understand the need to walk the walk and not just talk the talk.

light dawned. I asked myself, "Why do you want this binder twine! What if Philip does use it?" So when I went in to supper that night, Philip was there and I began, "Say, about that binder twine!" He hung his head, and mumbled, "Yes, Daddy." Then I said, "Philip, I've changed my mind. You can use that old binder twine any time you want. What's more all those tools out in the garage I've labeled 'No' – you go ahead and use them. I can buy new tools, but I can't buy new boys." There never was a sunrise like that smile. "Thanks, Daddy," he beamed. And guess what, Peter? He hasn't touched that binder since![7]

IN SUMMARY

The matter of fathers turning back to their children is a heart issue.

Mothers have been given influence. Fathers have been given authority.

As fathers, we occupy a God-given position and such a position bears God-given authority. We must realize the responsibility that comes with that position.

For almost three decades, many men have dropped out of their positions as protectors of that which is sacred. They have gone lethargically to their couches of ease, greed and passivity.

Being gentle like "a nurse" in our unconditional love is primary for all fathers. However, there is a progression from this gentle, feminine love to a more masculine love in Paul's epistle to the Thessalonians.

Exhortation is the first of three words that Paul uses in relation to his interaction with his spiritual children. An exhorting father is the best of all because he aims for the heart rather than the head of his children.

One of the greatest joys of an exhorting father is in building the character of his children and guiding them into full, meaningful lives. These fathers are generally standing close to their children with ready words of edification and encouragement.

An exhorting father takes facts and teaches his children how to walk them out in very practical ways, often outlining specifically what steps the child is to take.

An exhorting father communicates well with his children. He communicates hope and encouragement to a child when a problem arises. He keeps his eyes focused on the solution rather than on the problem. Accentuating the positive and eliminating the negative in his children's lives is fundamental to an exhorting father.

Exhorting fathers not only expect much from themselves personally, but they expect a lot from their children because they see the untapped potential within them. They motivate and encourage their children to reach for the highest and fulfill the best within themselves.

185

Chapter Eleven

Realizing our Position
Section II

I n addition to Paul's use of the word "exhortation" regarding his spiritual children, he also used two other words, "comfort" and "charge." Like the word "gentle," the word "comfort" is one of those feminine words that might seem to exclude the masculine. Yet, under the inspiration of the Holy Spirit, Paul stated that he first exhorted his children and then he comforted them. "The Comforter" is one of the names of the Holy Spirit in the New Testament, and this name is vitally important to all members of the body of Christ because of all it encompasses. In His role of comforter, the Holy Spirit comes alongside us to impart strength and hope, and to ease the grief or trouble we feel. With the Holy Spirit as our Guide, we fathers should seek to follow that example and comfort our children.

A Father's Comfort

One of the easy tasks for fathers is to supply the physical comforts of life, and there is an undeniable principle of connection in the Word of God between the meeting of physical needs and the ministry of comfort. When the angels appeared unto Abraham in the plains of Mamre, he instantly tried to minister to them by bringing water and saying, "I will fetch a morsel of bread, and comfort ye your hearts."[1] And in the book of Judges is the record of a Levite who lodged at his father-in-law's house after retrieving his run-away concubine. After four days, the Levite prepared to leave, but his father-in-law sought to detain him: "Comfort thine heart with a morsel of bread, and afterward go your way."[2] In a real sense, then, we fathers can comfort our children when we provide the "morsel of bread" upon the table for their consumption. This natural tendency to provide physical comfort for our children is necessary, yet it can become the main focus of our attention. We must provide the physical comforts without pulling ourselves away in the meantime; it is our presence that offers the greatest comfort to our children. Obviously, there is more involved in the word "comfort" and its scriptural relevance to our roles as fathers who comfort our children. So, apart from physical provision, how do we comfort our children?

The Bible speaks also of being "comforted in . . . affliction" in the book of Psalms.[3] The verse goes on to say, "thy word hath quickened me." Similarly, a father can, simply by the use of words, quicken his children and comfort them in their affliction. The word "affliction" connotes anything that puts a strain on a child's power of endurance. Children can be afflicted in numerous ways including embarrassment and even distress in their relationships with peers. Fathers should be careful to remember their own childhood days and the numerous sorrows and afflictions that they faced. Also, it is wise to realize that the intensity of afflictions upon children today is probably double or triple that of their fathers in their childhood years. The forces of evil that lurk in our culture, ready to afflict the innocence of children, are numerous and pervasive. Fathers must stand ready to comfort their children. They must watch carefully to notice when their children face situations in which they need comfort. Then, of course, fathers must provide that comfort.

As I studied the scriptural word for comfort, an interesting thought surfaced. Most of us have lain upon our beds at night needing comfort at some point in our lives. The bed is often a place of refuge from our emotional afflictions and discouragements. More pillow cases are probably stained with tears than any other fabric in the world. Job, probably more than any other character in the Bible, is a picture of affliction, and during his affliction, he gave testimony about his bed being a place of comfort to him: "My bed shall comfort me, my couch shall ease my complaint."[4] As fathers and mothers, we would be wise and make it a habit of saying good-night to our children as they lie upon their beds. Those moments before going to sleep may present the most valuable opportunity we have that day for comforting our children.

In comforting our children, we need to be aware that there will come a time in the future when we will not be there personally to comfort them. Because of this fact, we need to teach them how to find comfort for themselves in the scriptures. In Paul's epistle to the Romans, he taught them that one of the means of having hope was through the comfort of the scriptures: "For whatsoever things were written aforetime were written for our learning, that we through patience and comfort of the scriptures might have hope."[5]   It is a wise father who trains his child to turn to the scriptures for comfort. In doing this, he gives them the legacy of hope that comes only through the comfort of the scriptures.

A Father's Charge

The final word that Paul used in reference to his spiritual children was "charge." He reminded them that he, "charged every one of you, as a father doth his children."[6] The natural question to this comment is, "How does a father go about "charging" his children?" The answer is found in the Greek word translated "charge."

More pillow cases are stained with tears than any other fabric in the world.

It implies that Paul "testified" to his spiritual children or "witnessed" to them. The scriptural sense of the word is that just as Paul proclaimed the truths of the gospel to the Romans, he also testified or bore witness to the power of those truths. The Greek word used in the passage is mainly subjective, having to do with the apostle Paul's personal experience rather than the objective idea of a message or the thing which he preached.

Therefore, a father's "charge" to his children should in reality be his testimony before them, and it should be on a subjective level. In other words, it should be in his walking the walk rather than his talking the talk. A father's witness must exhibit the power of the truths which he speaks as he demonstrates them in his life in front of his children. And this truth points back to what I noted earlier in the objectives of training. Our children learn from our examples more than they learn from what we say. Our example is our "charge" to them. Also, there is significance in the progression of the words that the apostle Paul used in his epistle. Our "charge," or testimony, follows exhortation and comfort. In fact, it is the exhortation and comfort of our children that partially enable us to witness before our children.

Earlier I stated that the private life of former President Bill Clinton and politics did not enter into the scope of this book. While I still maintain this to be true, the political situation nevertheless placed the fathers of America at a crossroads. If we believe in a sovereign God, then we must believe that that situation did not catch Him unawares as He sits upon His throne. Why then did the Lord allow the situation to arise? It would appear that the president had numerous times in his life to make different choices as a husband and a father. It would also appear that he acted without respect to his position and with no regard whatsoever to his testimony involving the children of America. During that dark time in our history there were reports of young boys who freely grabbed the off-limits parts of the bodies of young girls as a result of the example set by the president. When taken to the principal's office and reprimanded, the reply from these boys was, "If the president does it, why can't we?"

As fathers, we need to carefully observe the cultural crossroads at which we now find ourselves in America.

We cannot fall into the group of Christians who point fingers of accusation and condemnation. Neither can we sit passively back and think that things will take care of themselves. God has brought us to this moral cross-roads in America. What shall we do? What can we do to resolve this problem?

Perhaps one of the most alarming things to surface during the Grand Jury trial of President Clinton was the apathy of Americans who were not outraged at immorality. William Bennett's book, *The Death of Outrage*, addressed this indifference to immorality. While the book chronicles the events surrounding the president from January of 1998 until a few days before he testified before the Grand Jury in August of 1998, Bennett's premise is that moral outrage has died in America. The man who held the highest office in our country plunged us as a nation into a scandal regarding sexual immorality; yet as a nation we justified it, claiming, "Everybody does it." At the conclusion of Bennett's book, he adds a postscript. It should be personally addressed to every father in America:

> Throughout this book, I have explained why I believe the arguments made in defense of Bill Clinton are harmful to our national life. In the end, perhaps the most important residue of the Clinton scandals will be pedagogical; that is, the lessons they will teach children–and their parents, too. If the arguments are left standing, if the justifications are left intact, it is worth considering the lessons that will be taught . . .
>
> 1. Character in our president doesn't matter. It's the economy, stupid.

2. Some powerful people are above the law. They don't need to play by the rules.

3. Adultery is no big deal. It's commonplace. Europeans don't care about it; neither should we.

4. It's okay to lie under oath.

5. It's okay to grope women as long as you eventually take no for an answer.

6. It's okay to close your eyes to wrongdoing when it's your own powerful friends and political allies who have done wrong.

7. [Many] people engage in misconduct, so it doesn't matter if you do, too. Everybody does it. This is especially true in politics.

8. A person hasn't really done anything wrong unless he's been convicted in a court of law.

9. If you do something wrong and people question you about it, do not voluntarily step forward, admit wrongdoing, and take responsibility. Instead, consider doing any or all of the following:

> Promise to give them answers soon; then stall by giving evasive answers or no answers at all. Maybe they'll get tired and drop it.

> Just feign ignorance about what you've done. Say [that] you don't know what happened, [that] you just don't have the facts.

> Attack those who are raising the questions. Try [to] dig up dirt on them. And intimidate them if you can.

Play down and make fun of their concerns.

Claim that people are conspiring to make you look guilty.

Don't explain yourself.

10. The ends justify the means."[7]

The Moral Outrage of a Father

Flying throughout the country to go to my evangelistic meetings offers me a great deal of time to contemplate different things. Thinking back on the moral situation regarding the president, I have lately wondered if William Bennett is not right.

Has moral outrage died among the citizens of our country? More importantly, has moral outrage died among

> *Has moral outrage died among the citizens of the United States of America?*

the men of our country? Anthropologists and psychologists tell us that within the belly of each man beats the heart of a warrior. Where are our spiritual warriors? Have we lived in a culture of immorality for so long that it did not outrage us to have a president who so blatantly lied? One of the most troubling symptoms of our sick culture is the absence of moral outrage in the American public. God forbid that we allow this to remain!

Where are our heroes? Where are the spiritual warriors who are morally outraged and will enter the arena to wrestle with evil in its many disguises? It is my belief that God the Father still delights in fiercely strong spiritual warriors. Where are the powerful men, rich in mercy and contemplative judgment, yet still possessing righteous thunder and lightning? These are not dispassionate spectators who sit idly by and do nothing. Neither are these the critics who point their fingers, only to retreat back into their caves of cowardice.

A hero's path in the world is bound to be filled with conflict. Overcoming these conflicts is partially what makes a man a hero. Our eyelids must not close when we see immorality, violence, disease, suffering, and injustice. Instead, outrage should rise up within us, and our hearts should hear the call to arms. The sense of desecration in knowing that immorality seeks to devour our children should prompt us, from deep within our beings, to run to the front line. Within the heroic male identity lies an instinctive capacity for outrage against evil and for protection of loved ones. This moral outrage should call us forth from our lethargy and passiveness.

We must guard against self-righteousness in our "holy war" against immorality.

As fathers, we are obliged to defend the sacred. We are called to be protectors of the powerless (our children) and healers of the broken (our prodigal children). This obligation is a part of our "charge" to our children. We are to be their heroes. How can we claim to be children of the Warrior of the ages and not experience outrage at the immorality that exists within our nation?

These are terrible times in our nation's history. Yet they are wonderful times because they afford us the opportunity to step up to the plate and hit a home run for the Lord. He is looking for a "few good men." Will you be one? We are involved in a holy war of the spirit that is against immorality, suffering, greed, bureaucracies and governments that desecrate the foundations upon which this nation was built. Our children desperately need their fathers to be heroes. The virtues of the warrior—fierceness, fortitude, daring, courage and cunning— are needed today as much as when they were once used to protect and defend the tribe. And the most exalted of heroes is he who has fulfilled a purpose that transcends his own. This kind of hero understands and senses that he is used for a divine purpose without falling into the hazardous pit of self-righteousness in all its different forms.

There is one final important caveat to consider with regard to the charge we provide for our children. If we become our children's heroes, who go to the front line, then we must guard against self-righteousness in our "holy war" against immorality. It creeps easily into our judgments. It was easy for us to condemn a president whose sins were televised before the American public, yet any one of us could fall victim to lust as we observe the attractive woman sitting two desks in front of us at our place of business. In order to guard against self-righteousness, the father-hero, the spiritual warrior, must practice the discipline of perpetual repentance. This is the subject of our next chapter.

IN SUMMARY

The second word outlined in Paul's letter to his

spiritual children is the word "comfort." One of the foremost ways of comforting our children is providing food for them.

The scriptures outline different aspects of comfort that a father might provide for his children. He should be a comfort to them during their times of affliction and at night when they get into bed, where the pressures of the day tend to be released. And he should teach them the comfort of the scriptures that will offer them hope.

The third word, translated as "charged" in the King James Version, entails the meaning of "testify," or "witness." A father's "charge" to his children is his godly testimony or witness lived out before them. In other words, fathers should walk the walk and not just talk the talk before their children.

Our purpose is not to condemn or judge any person, but it is to call all men everywhere to exhibit a moral outrage against scandals such as the one that has occurred in our nation's capital.

We must carefully consider the moral crossroads we face as a nation.

We must individually ask ourselves, "Am I part of the reason that moral outrage has died in America?"

We must rush to the front lines of the battle for our culture and be wise heroes of our children.

Chapter Twelve

Resolving our Problems

The real father-hero whom I discussed earlier is the one who courageously faces the unknown. He hears the call and responds, not knowing exactly where his journey will take him or what obstacles he may meet along the way. Men like this one are the men and fathers who are undaunted by the impossible. They firmly believe that all things are possible with God. These heroes put on their courage, shoulder their doubts and start down the path. They acknowledge that they are vulnerable, but in knowledge they realize that they "can do all things through Christ which strengtheneth [them]."[1] America cries out for such heroes.

In Chapter 11, I said that if we go to the front line, then we must guard against self-righteousness in our "holy war" against immorality since self-righteousness can so easily creep into our judgments. In order for us to guard against the pitfall of self-righteousness, we, the father-heroes, the spiritual warriors, must practice the discipline of perpetual repentance. This perpetual repentance will be principal in our attempt to "resolve our problems" both in our nation and within our families. And this is a matter of importance for both fathers and mothers because resolving our problems is going to take a united effort by both.

Perpetual Repentance

The matter of repentance can be distinguished in three elements. The first one is the intellectual element. With this intellectual element of repentance, we experience a change of view. We recognize sin and realize our own personal guilt. Likewise, we see sin's defilement upon our lives; we experience *epinosis hamartia*, or "knowledge of sin." If this knowledge of sin is not accompanied by the next two elements of repentance, however, it may simply manifest itself in our lives as a fear of punishment, while we remain devoid of any real hatred of sin.

> *We must practice the discipline of perpetual repentance if we seek to resolve the problems in our nation and within our families.*

The second element of repentance is an emotional one. With this element, we have a change of feeling that may manifest itself in sorrow for the sin we have committed against a holy and just God. This emotional element of repentance is seen in

200

King David's life when his sin with Bathsheba was exposed: "Wash me thoroughly from mine iniquity, and cleanse me from my sin. Create in me a clean heart, O God; and renew a right spirit within me. Deliver me from blood-guiltiness, O God, thou God of my salvation: and my tongue shall sing aloud of thy righteousness."[2]

The emotional element of David's repentance is quite evident in this psalm, yet if he had not moved beyond this emotional element, he would have only experienced what is known as *lupe tou kosmou* or "sorrow of the world," which manifests itself in remorse and despair and is sincere, but it does not view sin from God's perspective. This type of repentance is contrasted with *lupe kata theou*, which signifies "godly sorrow." Paul made the distinction between these two forms of repentance in his second epistle to the Corinthians: "For godly sorrow worketh repentance to salvation not to be repented of: but the sorrow of the world worketh death."[3]

This "sorrow of the world" repentance is apparent in two other places in the New Testament. When the rich young ruler came to the Lord wanting to follow Him, the Lord told him the sacrifice that he must pay to become a disciple, "and when he [rich young ruler] heard this, he was very sorrowful: for he was very rich."[4] He was truly "very sorrowful," but he was also "very rich." The Greek word indicates that the rich young ruler experienced genuine emotional sorrow, but it was not the "godly sorrow" that viewed his life from God's perspective. It was not enough for him to forsake his riches and follow the Lord.

This same Greek word (meaning "sorrow of the world") is also used to describe Judas after his betrayal of Jesus: "Then Judas, when he saw that he was condemned, repented himself, and brought again the thirty pieces of silver to the chief priests and elders, saying, I have sinned in that I have betrayed the innocent blood."[5] The word implies that Judas had emotional regret, but there was not true repentance of turning from his sin toward God.

From the scriptural position, then, it seems that this emotional repentance is not the ultimate goal and final purpose of the Lord. Instead, the Lord seeks to move us beyond this emotional level and into his presence, allowing us to see our sin from His perspective.

The third and final aspect of repentance is found in the volitional element. This consists of a change of purpose in our lives and comes about when we go beyond the intellectual and the emotional element of recognizing our sin. We experience an inward turning away from sin and a recoiling, remorseful sorrow over how our sin has affected the heart of the Father. In our godly sorrow, we offer not a shred of defense regarding our sin. We take complete responsibility and do not blame others for the exposure of our sin; and we are shamefully and inwardly grieved because of it.

Mothers and Fathers

Sincere repentance is a complex process and involves a radical reckoning with our own hearts. And it is absolutely the first step in resolving problems in our personal lives, within our families and in our nation. It involves going before the Lord, opening our hearts to Him and asking His Holy Spirit to come in and search our hearts.

In the context of David's psalm mentioned previously, he gives us a pattern of repentance. First, somewhere between his years of tending his father's sheep and becoming king of Israel, he recognized and accepted the fact that he was born a sinner, as the passage clearly indicates: "Behold, I was shapen in iniquity; and in sin did my mother conceive me."[6] Although we all realize this truth, we are often guilty of trying to cover up or defend our sinful nature. This defensiveness validates evidence that we have not truly completely repented, and we remain trapped in the first stage of repentance if we go no further. We have an intellectual or head knowledge that we have sinned, but we do not view our sin from God's perspective.

David was sincere in his repentance, however, and went beyond the intellectual and emotional aspects, stating that God, "desirest truth in the inward parts: and in the hidden part thou shalt make me to know wisdom."[7] If David were alive today, he would understand that God would not be interested in all the lessons he could teach in Sunday school or how much money he could give to the local church if there were unconfessed sin in his life. David realized that God wants truth in the inward parts of our lives.

We must experience a radical reckoning with our own hearts regarding repentance.

With this in mind, we must ask ourselves, "Have I done this yet? Have I personally asked the Lord to give me the gift of repentance for sin in my life?" He is a good God, and it is His will to give us repentance. As a matter of fact, the scriptures tell us that "the goodness of God leadeth [us] to repentance."[8] We need not fear repentance; we should allow God's goodness to lead us to it.

Understanding and applying this principle of repentance is imperative to us as parents. Until we experience this personally as individuals so that it can then flow unhindered into the daily workings of our families, we cannot hope to fight effectively the cultural immorality that corrupts our children. It will do little good to have moral outrage without the ground of repentance beneath us, because without the humility that results from repentance, we risk becoming self-righteous. We can become guilty of pointing fingers of condemnation rather than killing the Goliath of immorality in our nation. Our genuine, personal repentance is the stone that God will use to slay this giant. I cannot stress this enough.

Now permit me to be very direct. Mom, do you want to establish some traditions that will give your daughter her identity? Dad, do you seek to teach your son the ways of God? Parents, do you want to protect your children's consciences from the contamination of our perverse culture? Then pray for personal repentance for yourself.

Mom, do you want to obtain the objectives of giving your children a spiritual, emotional and social legacy? Dad, do you want to reach the objective of giving your children a physical and moral legacy? You will accomplish this best by sincerely seeking God's face and asking Him to lead you to repentance. Do this sincerely. God will not fail to answer such prayers.

Once we have tasted the fruit of repentance and felt the inner cleansing of its work, we will see the need for perpetual repentance. May we, on a daily basis, go before the throne of our great God and ask for His mercy upon us, upon our families and upon our nation. We must ask Him daily to search our hearts and cleanse them for our sakes, and for the sake of our children and our nation. Mom, Dad, please do this for the sake of your children.

As individuals, as families, and as a nation, we cannot ask God to go against His own ways, against the pattern He has established for us in His Word. Unless we repent, then we cannot ask Him to kill this giant of immorality whose shadow covers our land. Repentance is the solution to our problem. One particular passage from God's Word is uniquely applicable to the past two decades as God's clarion call to his people to repent. The passage records God's words to Solomon after the dedication of the Temple.

> And the Lord appeared to Solomon by night, and said unto him, I have heard thy prayer, and have chosen this place to myself for an house of sacrifice. If I shut up heaven that there be no rain, or if I command the locusts to devour the land, or if I send pestilence among my people;

> If my people, which are called by my name, shall humble themselves, and pray, and seek my face, and turn from their wicked ways; then will I hear from heaven, and will forgive their sin, and will heal their land.[9]

This is a familiar verse to all of us, and there is a growing movement among Christians to humble themselves, to pray, to seek God's face and to turn from their sins. And we are beginning just now to feel the power of this movement toward repentance. Thousands are fasting and praying for the Lord to heal our land, and many have made sacrifices. We may never know the extent to which these people should be credited for holding back the total destruction of our nation, but we know that many more must join in until our numbers swell enough to be heard in the heavens, until God in His sovereignty answers our prayers and heals our land.

Sacrifices of Mom and Dad

Because I live in the real world, I recognize that there are less than ideal situations and relationships in our Christian homes. I understand that there are countless thousands of single mothers having to be both Mom and "Dad" to their children. I acknowledge the high divorce rate among my fellow Christians, and it has not escaped my attention that there is far too much apathy and passivity among Christian men and that they often allow women to carry the spiritual burden of their families. Although I concede all these things, I nevertheless present the "ideal" means of resolving our problems. Regardless of our situation, we must look beyond excuses and see that these ideal means can be altered to fit each personal situation.

Whether male or female, we must step forward and determine to pay the price to solve the problems in our families and in our nation. Obviously, this price will certainly involve sacrifice. The necessary sacrifice may be as small as losing an extra hour or two of sleep a night, or it may be more costly. It may cost a vocation or relationships with extended family members. If we plan to see our problems solved, we must prepare to sacrifice whatever it takes to do so. Also, some of us may never live to see the results of our sacrifice because what we seek to undertake could take decades before it becomes readily visible within our families or our nation. Are we

206

willing to make this sacrifice?" Are we willing to be the ones who do not need to see the instant results but will begin to dig down deep and build a foundation for the characters and souls of our children? Are we willing to step forward and rebuild the foundations of America? Has your moral outrage been touched enough that you will sacrifice whatever it takes to stand against the tide of immorality, to protect the consciences of our children, and to restore the conscience of America? Yes? I pray so.

The cycle of immorality must be broken in our nation. As responsible adults and Christian parents, we can no longer tolerate the evil within our culture that seeks to destroy our children. If the cycle must be broken, and it must, then it must begin with us. It must start with our generation. We dare not wait any longer.

The cycle of immorality must be broken in our nation. As responsible adults and Christian parents, we can no longer tolerate the evil within our culture that seeks to destroy our children.

One of my favorite eras in American history is the World War II era. I particularly enjoy the study of decisive battles. An outstanding truth regarding Normandy was that someone had to be the first to hit the sand when we stormed the beaches, and those soldiers knew they would be sacrificed. Yet they did it in order to secure the victory for our country. Those soldiers who sacrificed themselves were the true heroes of that battle. They unselfishly gave their lives as a sacrifice for freedom. This is what I am asking you to do,

Mother. This is what I am asking you to do, Father. Will you sacrifice yourself for the sake of others, for the sake of your children and your grandchildren? You may never be given a white marker on your grave as a reminder that you stormed the beaches of Immorality, but Heaven will mark your sacrifice.

In the end, we must ask ourselves one question: Do I really care about the condition of America's morals? And someone, someplace, somehow must count the cost and be willing to pay it. For most of us, the cost might simply be relinquishing our pride and putting on the cloak of humility. Some of us may only be called upon to sacrifice our selfish ambitions or materialistic greed in order to be led to repentance, as many mothers who have sacrificed lucrative paychecks and stayed home in order to assure that their children will be given good spiritual and moral legacies. And we must remember that repentance must be perpetual. In order to break the cycle of degeneration in our country, we must maintain a perpetual repentance and a constant willingness to sacrifice. Are we willing to pay the price and be the true heroes for our children and grandchildren, for our nation?

IN SUMMARY

The real father hero courageously faces the unknown. He not only hears the call, but he responds as well. He is undaunted by the impossible because he believes all things are possible through God.

If we are to resolve our problems as individuals,

as families, and as a nation, we must practice perpetual repentance.

There are three elements to repentance. The first is an intellectual element through which we experience a change of view and consists mainly of fear of punishment rather than hatred of sin.

The second element of repentance is emotional. This element manifests itself through a change of feeling and the sorrow we have regarding our sins. It is mostly seen as regret and is referred to in the Bible as the "sorrow of the world."

The "sorrow of the world" was the term used in reference to the rich young ruler who was very sorrowful. He was very rich and did not want to give up his riches to follow Jesus. This "sorrow of the world" is also used in connection with Judas after he had betrayed the Lord.

The third element of repentance is volitional. This type of repentance is referred to as "godly sorrow" and it consists of a change of purpose in our lives and is an inward turning away from sin.

Mothers and fathers must first experience true repentance before any personal, family, or national problem can be resolved. David's repentance in Psalm 51 outlines this true type of repentance.

Mothers and fathers will have to make sacrifices before resolution can occur.

PART IV
PAIN OF
THE PRODIGAL

Chapter Thirteen

Parenting the Potential Prodigal

The lengthy Prescription for Parenting was written with the hope that some parents might be able to read the next few chapters, shake their heads in sympathy, and yet never experience the terrible pain involved with a prodigal child. However, scores of parents have tasted the salt of their endless tears because their children have left their families and left their faith. I addressed some of the positive means of avoiding this in Part II, Prescription for Parenting, yet the fact is that in spite of all that a parent may do, there may still come that time when a child turns his back and walks away. The first step in dealing with this heart-breaking truth lies in finding the answers to the question, "Why?" Why do our children become prodigals?

From the beginning of recorded history in the Bible,

people have wandered away from God. One of my favorite hymns includes the line, "Prone to wander, Lord, I feel it. Prone to leave the God I love." Within each of us is the tendency to wander away from the Lord, and life can present numerous opportunities to do so at any age. But what is it that causes children, especially teenagers, to reject the faith of their parents? Is the lure of the world so strong upon our children that God's hand cannot reach them? Do peer pressures pull our children away from us? Whatever the causes, and we will discuss them, there are few situations that can cause greater heartache to a parent than the trauma of a prodigal child.

As I travel throughout the United States, these questions are asked of me by more mothers than any other: How can this happen? How can the gospel of Jesus Christ suddenly lose its appeal to my son? How can my daughter think that things of the Lord are suddenly so repulsive that she goes against her family and her Christian friends? She seems to want to get away from anything to do with the Lord.

Obviously, these questions cannot be answered in a few simple words. My answer to parents is scattered throughout the contents of this book. It involves laying a firm foundation as wisely as possible; making certain that your children are given the spiritual, emotional, social, physical and moral legacies they need to live abundant lives; remembering the requirement that a child must see the reality of Jesus Christ in his parents' lives; and walking in perpetual repentance. These are all keys that can hinder the enemy's attempts to break into a child's life with the intent to destroy him.

Again, even Christian children leave home. Let's examine some of the things that might precede the prodigal child's departure. It is an interesting fact that when people come to know the Lord when they are adults, very few of them leave their faith. In comparison, many children who were raised in Christian homes turn their backs and walk away. This might be a warning signal for us as Christian parents to take a serious inventory regarding the fundamentals of our parenting. I have stated several times that it is never too late to implement some of the things discussed in the Prescription for Parenting chapters. If your children are teenagers, you may need to make some wise adjustments, so in this section I will restate and add to some of the foundations we discussed earlier.

Potential Prodigals Are Angry

From listening to many young prodigals, I have learned that there are several fundamental reasons why potential prodigals eventually turn their backs and walk away from their families. Some of these young people are openly hostile and extremely bitter. Many have embraced a lifestyle that sends parents crying to either a pastor or family and friends. And often they become involved in sexual promiscuity, drugs, alcohol, pornography or a dozen other destructive lifestyles that can destroy all but the strongest faith of any parent.

Not all of these young prodigals are angry, but certainly the majority of them are. It seems to me that the anger of a young teenager ought to be the first signal to a parent that there is trouble in paradise. Seeing anger in a young person should throw up a red flag, signalling that there is another message beneath that anger. We cannot

215

afford to brush the anger of our young people off with the comment that it is "just something he is going through." Neither can we afford to ignore anger that is hidden behind a smile of false obedience. If we really take the time to listen to our children, a valid reason for their frustration will surface.

Two types of anger are often manifested in teens. There is the aggressive, blatant anger that few of us have difficulty recognizing, and then there is the passive anger that is hidden behind a smile of compliance. Teens with passive anger do not want to be labeled as troublemakers or rebellious, so they hide their anger from others, but it is there just the same. Many teens have received either a subliminal or an outright message that saying anything negative and expressing any type of anger is sinful. When a child is passive in his anger, it comes out in different forms, such as never completing a task he has been assigned. He will "accidentally forget" to complete the task given to him. If he is confronted, he will plead ignorance. Some will offer weak, half-hearted apologies just to avoid appearing rebellious, but inwardly they are not truly sorry. A parent must not be fooled by his child's silent communications. He may be seething with anger, but controlling its expression through "proper" responses. Parents often deceive themselves when a child reacts with passive anger rather than outspoken, obvious anger.

Many children who become prodigals have actually been raised in Christian homes by Christian parents. What has happened?

Teens with an aggressive form of anger have no problem with allowing their parents to know precisely how they feel. However, when a young person blatantly throws his anger at his parent, he may actually be shouting at the top of his voice, "Will somebody pay attention to what I need?" Very often, the teenager is simply asking to be treated fairly. Many angry teenagers often feel ignored. They feel unappreciated by most of the family. Hundreds of teenagers display anger simply because they feel like no one is listening to them or no one really cares what they think.

Just as often, teens become angry because they have been given a certain amount of freedom and independence which is suddenly snatched away from them. Their anger screams out: "I can control my own life, and I need someone to support me in the fact that I can make my own decisions!" Once a teenager has tasted the freedom and power of independence, it becomes extremely difficult for him to relinquish that independence. Teens learn to love the control they have over their own lives, and when they make unwise choices, as all teens do, they become angry if they are not given the reassurance that they are capable of making wise choices.

Many parents also face young persons whose anger proclaims, "I want to live my own life and I want to do it now!" Patience has never been a great attribute of a teenager. They have one speed and that is acceleration to do what they want, when they want to do it. For the first time in their lives, adolescents see that a new world of opportunities and experiences awaits them. They resist anyone who tries standing in their path.

Again, as I have observed the lives of these potential

prodigals, and I emphasize "potential," I have seen that the vast majority of them are filled with anger. In most cases, there is no relief valve through which this anger can escape without bringing on the condemnation of parents. The examples above are only a few hidden messages that are concealed beneath a young person's visible anger. When a teenager becomes sullen and angry, parents must not ignore it and think it is only a passing phase! Instead, they should face it directly and deal with it carefully.

Two particular guidelines are especially effective in handling anger when it surfaces.

1. An angry teenager cannot spit and swallow at the same time. Have you ever tried spitting and swallowing at the same time? Try it right now. Try spitting something out of your mouth and swallowing something else at the same time? It is absolutely impossible. When a teenager is spitting out his anger, it is impossible for him to swallow down a sermon or instructions from his parents regarding what he should do; yet for some reason, most of us think we have to preach or instruct our children when they articulate their anger. Very often, he just needs to vent his anger, to get it out.

Earlier, I stressed the need to listen to our children. Anger presents one of those crucial times when we, as parents, must listen. If we start trying to get our children to swallow something that they cannot swallow at that particular moment then, in essence, we are shoving that anger back down their throats. The anger that we refused to hear, may turn out to cause the first step a child takes in walking away. Anger is not pretty. Sometimes it can even be frightening if it

218

is coming from a strong-willed, choleric personality. But fasten your seat belts, Mom and Dad, and just listen. Really listen. Your child may have a valid complaint, and your helping to remedy it will do wonders for the parent-child relationship.

2. Try to avoid the deception that you can completely purge away all of a teenager's anger at one time. The initial reaction that most parents have to a teenager's anger is to put the lid on it and tell him to shelve it. Parents see anger as a defiant behavior that has to be "nipped in the bud" as Barney admonished on The Andy Griffith Show. Barney meant well, but "nipping it in the bud" might not be the most productive thing to do when dealing with angry teenagers. Countless thousands of parents have disciplined their teenagers in response to their anger. Thinking they were teaching a valuable lesson and tackling the problem at its onset, many of these parents have witnessed later explosions of even more anger in their rebellious teenager. In his book, *The Angry Teenager*, Dr. William Carter offers some guidelines to parents when they are communicating with an angry teenager.

> Diffuse a potentially explosive situation between yourself and your teen by walking away from likely confrontations. A teenager who does not have a verbal sparring partner is more likely to let "hot" emotions pass . . . it is sometimes better to walk away from a certain verbal slugfest. His defiance is his way of asking for a fight he knows he can win. By trying to overpower him, the parent may win the battle, but lose the war. A teenager is fully aware of his parents' frustration tolerance.

Focus attention on things you can control, specifically your own emotional reaction. Viewing the teen's behavior objectively allows you to "hear" the hidden messages the young person is trying to send to you. If you feel your defiant teen is asking for greater independence, give him independence in things he is likely to handle appropriately. If he is stating feelings of frustration over a weak self-image, make efforts to boost his worth through positive interaction. One stark reality of dealing with an angry teenager is that he cannot be forced to do what he has made up his mind not to do. Your teen knows this and willingly takes advantage of situations that give him a competitive edge. But the good news is that an emotionally-controlled parent can influence him in the right direction.

Talk with your teen after his intense emotions have passed. A frequent mistake we parents make in dealing with an angry teen is to vent our emotions when a crisis is in progress. Our own emotions may be as intense as the teen's. To release our emotions at their peak will likely escalate the tension. By waiting until the intensity of the moment has died down, healing communication is more probable.

Let your actions speak louder than your words. This age-old adage is well worn but true. An angry parent may make threats, accusations, or predictions in an angry tone of voice hoping to get through to an irresponsible young person. Instead of listening to the words of the adult, though, the teen will take note of how he caused the parent to go into emotional orbit. Ignoring his parent's words, he will take advantage of the chance to prey on the adult's emotions.

Take an inventory of your relationship with your teenager. Remember, through his anger a teenager may be stating that he is unsure of himself. The irony of this is that he may be so angry that the parent ignores his real need. Spending quality time with your teenager can take the edge off his anger.[1]

Please do not think for a moment that I am suggesting that because a teenager is angry that he will ultimately become a prodigal. That is not my intent in writing about an angry teenager. There is substantial evidence, however, that anger can be a preceding signal to communicate that a child feels strongly enough about his feelings to reject everything his parents have tried to teach him. If anger is not acknowledged and handled properly in the lives of our children, then it widens the door to influences that oppose everything that we have taught them, and some of the most influential pressures on our children are those that come from their peers.

Peer Pressure and Teenagers

Because of its intense influence, peer pressure has been the subject of countless polls and statistical studies. Also, parents and teens alike admit that it is peer pressure that can be the primary cause of sexual promiscuity, rebellion, drug use and violence among young people. And parents readily admit that the peer pressure their teens experience is like a giant tidal wave unleashing its destructive power and washing away everything they have sought to build into their children.

An interesting fact about peer pressure is that while it has gotten a bad reputation because of being the motivation behind a teenager's defiant attitude, it can also be positive. Peers can motivate one another to do good as well as evil. Generally, however, we only hear of the negative aspects of peer pressure. Actually, it is an issue in all of our lives. It begins during early childhood, mainly during the school years, and it continues into our adult years. It just kind of explodes during the teen years; a fact parents should remember. This explosion is what has given peer pressure such bad publicity.

Parents readily admit that the peer pressure teens experience is often viewed like a giant tidal wave unleashing its destructive power and washing away everything they have built into their children.

Adolescents agree with their parents regarding peer pressure. They name it as the number one fueler of teenage defiance and rebellion against parents. However, parents and teens see the victims of peer pressure differently. Parents fear, because they see the changes that take place in the lives of their youth as a result of peer pressure. Their teen children, on the other hand, readily admit how peer pressure influences their friends while not believing that they are personally susceptible to pressure from their own peers. In their youthful way of reasoning, they believe they are above such pressure. They acknowledge that some of their friends have fallen beneath such pressures, but consider themselves immune. They, after all, know the difference between right and wrong—they think.

During the years when teens begin pulling away from their parents, they focus quite a bit on their independence. They are stretching themselves, and pulling away from parents is the first step to their independence. Being dependent, after all, is being young. What they fail to realize is that they have only attached their basically dependent natures to someone other than their parents: their peers. In spite of a teen's cry for independence, he actually makes the choice to remain dependent. He just switches from one support system to another. So in reality, the teen is saying, "I want to be independent of my family, but I still need some people I can cling to and be dependent on."

Teenagers seek independence from their parents, yet they remain very dependent upon their peers for approval.

Carrying the pattern of years of emotional dependency from their childhood, teens do not simply toss away the weight of this former dependency. Instead, they transfer their dependence from their parents to their peers, and the generation gap begins to make its appearance. Naturally, most teens do not view themselves as being emotionally dependent upon their peers. The observations of their parents about how dependent they are can broaden that gap if a good foundation has not been laid.

One of the objectives I mentioned earlier in providing a spiritual legacy was to lay a firm foundation in teaching children a biblical world view. If we do this when our children are young, we will count our blessings and thank God for the foresight when they are teens. Even teens who are raised with healthy, biblical foundations struggle through the quagmire of the adolescent years with questions like:

Who am I, anyway? What kind of person will I be?

Who is God? Do I have a relationship with Him? How can I make sense of the spiritual world?

What makes me feel the way I do physically? What's happening to my body? What do I do with my physical impulses?

Empty conversations or constant condemnations only succeed in pushing parents out of the circle of influence with their children.

What am I good at? Is it true what others say about me? What is my opinion of myself?

What stance will I take on social issues? Political matters? Why do people believe the way they do?

Do I have any real power in this world? What difference can one person make?[2]

These questions, whether verbalized or not, will be asked by teens, and most of them will generally seek the answers from other teens rather than from parents. Trying to find the answers to these kinds of questions from their peers might not be the wisest choice, but it will generally be their first choice. In their attempt to make sense of the world in which they live, they ally themselves to those who are their peers. The same teen who insists that he is acting independently from peer pressure is most generally dependent upon his friends to help him in his search for personal understanding. Sadly, in their youthful immaturity, teens do not realize that many of their peers do not have a clue as to the answers of these questions, and often, teens become sullen, angry, or manifest aggressive behavior when these questions go unanswered. With this in mind, it is important for parents to remain available and keep the lines of communication open.

Parental Understanding

Keeping the emotional bond between a parent and his teenager secure might not be an easy task. Some heavy-duty glue is a necessity for keeping us cemented to our children, and when peer pressure exerts its influence, that glue is understanding. Many parents should be able to reach back into their memories as teens and somewhat relate to what their teens are experiencing, although it might take quite a bit of mental stretching. Actually, many parents really do understand what their teens are feeling or understand why they do what they do. The problem arises when the parent fears sharing this with the teen.

A mother once told me, "I really do understand what my son is feeling, but if I tell him this I am afraid that he will think I am approving of his feelings. I felt the same way when I was a teenager, but I was wrong." The mother's fear that her understanding would somehow destroy her son was pretty groundless. She felt safer telling the son how he should feel and how he should think. Rather than cementing her son to her emotionally, she ultimately pushed him further away.

If we live transparent lives before our children, they can benefit from our experience, even if that experience was a mistake or a failure on our part. Children, especially teens, have an instinctive radar for sensing what is genuine. As parents, we must be willing to offer them the opportunity to learn from our experiences and our mistakes. If we truly understand, then we must not fear sharing that understanding with our adolescents. Empty conversations or constant condemnations only succeed in pushing parents out of the circle of influence with their children.

Dr. Carter outlines some valuable points for parents to recognize as peer pressure pushes its way deeper into the lives of their children.

Parents would do well to recognize that teen reliance on the peer group moves him closer to responsible adult living. Rather than block the teen's effort to shed his dependence on the family, parents are in a position to help the growing, but still immature, young person. Parents can stay connected with their teenager. Teens need not drift too far from the wisdom of adults to a negative peer group. Some guidelines are as follows:

> Recognize that a teenager needs a separate identity from his parents as he becomes his own person. Overreacting to the teen's need to try different roles only pushes him to continue to be different, if for no other reason than to make a stronger statement of independence.

> Continue to be a part of your teenager's support

226

system. Even though the opinion of other teenagers is ultimately important, your opinion will continue to count if you show an awareness of your teen's positive qualities. Make a point of frequently complimenting your teen.

Refrain from giving your opinion on relatively unimportant matters until your teenager asks for your views or is obviously open to your comments. Focus on showing your teenager you understand him. He will not mistake your understanding for agreement. Teens know their parents well enough to know their opinion on virtually any topic. As you demonstrate a willingness to listen to your teen, he will ask for your advice more frequently.

Gradually ease parental controls. When parents refuse to give control to teenagers, rebellion is increasingly likely. Rebellious teens do not trust adults and feel they have no one to turn to for direction but their peer group. Conversely, when parents give up control too quickly, teens tend to weave through adolescence like a runaway train. The teen may say he's having fun in life, but his lifestyle of reckless abandon will come to a screeching halt some day.

These are the years when the foundation you have laid will be tested. It will either crack and crumble or it will hold firmly through the storms.

Recognize that healthy communication is your best tool in building a powerful relationship with your teenager. As you talk with your teen about things of interest to him, the conversation will often drift to topics that have eternal significance. Well-timed comments, spoken with tact and understanding, leave a lasting impression on the teenager. Teens are quick to accept the views of a parent who communicates with acceptance and understanding.

Live a lifestyle that shows your teen what it means to be personally, socially, and spiritually fulfilled. Teenagers notice authentic traits of happiness in adults. They will want to know how to find that contentment. Young people who come from families that are well-rooted are less likely to try to look for shortcuts to happiness."[3]

Parenting a potential prodigal may be something to which we all wish we could be oblivious. We wish we could say that it is our neighbor's problem and not our own. We cannot imagine that our child would fall into the category of a prodigal. Still, in the culture in which we live, the reality of raising a prodigal has become very likely. And the flood of statistics tells us that leaving the faith of parents or getting into serious trouble generally happens during teen years through the early twenties. The decisions our children make during the time frame of thirteen to twenty-one are crucial. They can permanently shape a child's life.

These are the years when the foundation parents have laid will be tested. They will either crack and crumble or hold firmly. Putting our children first is especially crucial during this time frame. We must give ourselves and our time to our children. And we must be transparent and honest with them. It is amazing how they can see through us as parents. It is imperative that we communicate with them, and speak openly and honestly with them.

I have observed thousands of parents and teens in their relationships with each other. One consistent theme surfaces over and over again as I listen to both sides of a given problem. If teens perceive that their parents are resisting them or trying to obstruct their struggle for independence, then they are much less receptive to any wisdom that the parent seeks to share with them. If parents truly seek to listen to their adolescents and make an effort to see things through their teen's eyes, then a great deal of pressure to reject parental values is removed.

IN SUMMARY

If we use wisdom in parenting the potential prodigal, then we may avoid the heartache of parenting the prodigal. All of us, not just our children, are prone to wander away from the Lord.

Not all angry teenagers are potential prodigals. However, a teen's anger may be sending a message to parents that there is the grave possibility that they could become prodigals.

We need to learn to recognize the two forms of anger: passive anger and aggressive anger. Also, learning to recognize the hidden message behind anger is essential. If parents are to help their children through these troublesome years,

229

they must learn to deal with anger.

Parents should remember the two guidelines for dealing with anger when it surfaces. The first is that an angry teenager cannot spit and swallow at the same time.

The second guideline is to avoid thinking that parents can purge away all of a teenager's anger at one time.

Peer pressure has received a bad reputation because it can often be pinpointed as the thing which motivates children to go astray.

Parents and teens agree regarding the negative impact of peer pressure, but they have differing views on who is affected. Parents see their own child being affected, while he thinks it is others who are affected and not himself.

The time spent in helping your child to develop a world view will be greatly rewarded when he reaches his teen years.

Chapter Fourteen

Problems of the Prodigal

What actually happens in the lives of our children that causes them to reject the faith that we have tried so hard to instill in them? Completely answering this question could encompass a book, itself, but there are some key factors that present themselves when we try to understand this growing problem among our children.

I want to state at the very beginning that this chapter is intended to bring hope and not despair to the parent whose heart may have already been broken by a wandering child. As high as the statistics are regarding prodigals, there is also validation that a great many of them return home. Also, parents must not overly condemn themselves if a child has become a prodigal. Not all godly parents always succeed in securing all the cracks in the foundation. A prime example of this is Billy Graham's oldest child, Franklin. He rebelled against everything Billy Graham stood for until he was in his twenties. We must always remember that the Sovereign God still sits on His throne and has everything under control. What the Devil intends for evil and destruction regarding our children, the Lord will turn into good and restoration. We can also take comfort in the many ultimate victories, like the young Graham prodigal who returned home and now has a flourishing ministry.

My experience in dealing with teenagers has demonstrated two primary reasons as to why they become young prodigals. I do not say that these are the only reasons. I merely suggest these two because they seem to be the dominant reasons.

"Faith Just Didn't Work For Me."

These words have been both mumbled with embarrassment and growled in anger at me. Generally, there is also some guilt associated with such a confession. They tried it, they say. It just didn't work for me. Maybe I wasn't as spiritual as the others. They did give it a try, however. They went to Sunday school and listened to the sermons, but something just did not click during the time they were actively involved in the youth department.

Several reasons stand behind a teen's belief that faith did not work for him.

One reason is the inability to find answers to questions that eventually caused personal doubts. Many teens have theological questions, and they approach them from an academic viewpoint. When the questions were not answered to their satisfaction, they became disillusioned with church and church people. Another factor in this season of question is that it usually occurs during the years of high school or college when children spend much time away from their parents. Naturally, when a teen is questioning the issues of family faith, he will, in his genuine need to belong, turn to friends who do not embrace Christianity and listen to his friends' reasons why faith is foolish. Also, in secular colleges especially, finding professors who teach a Christian world view is rare. Contrary to that, most teach reasons to doubt things of the Lord. When a child does not seem to be able to find adequate answers, he concludes that faith just didn't work for him. Some even begin to pride themselves on the fact that they "live in the real world" and not the "make-believe world of Christianity."

Another reason a young prodigal may become disillusioned is because his faith is not really authentic. He tries to conform to what his parents and his pastor tell him, but everything proves to be empty. Rather than making his own spiritual choices or authenticating his own faith, he follows along with what everyone else does. Then, when a crisis, whether small or large, enters into his life, his faith collapses. Why? He had never personally embraced the ways of the Lord for himself.

If a child has been taught a Christian world view, then it is difficult to depart from it when he is older.

"I Want More Than What Christianity Can Offer."

While some teens find Christianity

ineffective, others find it insufficient. This generally means they want more material possessions, but it can range from material possessions to popularity among peers. In their attempt to succeed in life, many of these young prodigals focus on what they know does not line up with Christianity. Others simply drift away. The lure of the world dances before them, and they are enticed and then drawn away by the love of the world.

Unlike the disillusioned prodigal, this teen may have actually experienced an authentic faith at one time. He has just slowly drifted away and ended up with a secular viewpoint rather than a Christian world view. His desires and what he wants in life have became larger than things of the Lord, and slowly, the things of the Lord have faded from his conscience. Gradually he changes his mind about what is important to him.

The Prodigal Son

Obviously, the best story about a prodigal is the one recorded in the Bible, and Jesus' parable about the prodigal son is an all-time favorite of mine. Although it is tragic, it ends in hope. This parable especially shows that the heart of the heavenly Father greatly desires restoration, and its beauty is seen in the father's love for his son. It has become known as "the parable of the prodigal son," yet it is the father who is mentioned twelve times in the fifteenth chapter of Luke's gospel. It could be more appropriately titled "the parable of the searching father."

In the parable, the father had two sons. All of his possessions had been theirs as they both grew up and lived in his home. The younger son decided that he no longer wanted to be under his father's authority, so he demanded the inheritance that would have been his anyway. He knew the inheritance was to be his; he simply did not want to wait for his father to die. Apparently, the father acknowledged his son's desires, because he divided his property between his two sons. His younger son then moved away to a distant land.

The prodigal not only left his father's authority, but he also left his father's fellowship. He wanted to be out from under the restraining influence of his father, so he chose to submit no longer to his father's authority. Then, squandering all of the wealth of his inheritance on things of the world, the prodigal soon found himself alone, without money and with very little food. To add to his problems, a famine came into the land where he lived. He found himself reduced to poverty. In order to feed himself, he took a job as a servant in the foreign land. It was his job to feed the pigs, and apparently, they were fed better than he was.

The prodigal not only left his father's authority, but he left his father's fellowship as well.

With the stench of the pig pen swirling up into his nostrils, the prodigal son remembered when his life had been much better. The Bible says that "when he came to himself," he decided to go back home.[1] In his mind, he began developing a plan of confession to his father. He was going to confess that he had "sinned against heaven, and before [his father]."[2] Then he decided that he would make a proposition to his father: "I am no more worthy to be called thy son: make me as one of thy hired servants."[3] The prodigal was not going to ask his father to restore him to the full privileges of being a son. Broken and humbled, he planned to work as a servant until he could demonstrate his trustworthiness to his father. With this in mind, he rose up and started for his father's house. But his father saw him before he reached home.

This is the portion of the parable that makes it such a treasured story. We read, "But when he was yet a great way off, his father saw him, and had compassion, and ran, and fell on his neck, and kissed him."[4] The father was standing, watching for his son, and he waited daily for his return. The key to the verse, however, is that while the son was yet a great way off, the father saw him.

I cannot stress to you enough, mother and father, that you must see your prodigal coming home. And you must see him coming home while he is yet a great way

We must see our prodigal child while he is yet a great way off.

off. This seeing does not mean visualization in the sense that the New Age teaches it. This seeing is an act of faith, but biblical faith cannot work apart from the Word of God. There must first be a promise. Only then will we be able to see our prodigal trudging down the road that leads home. When we have a promise, we will be able actually to see our prodigal although he is yet a great way off, and it will be just as real as the day when he actually returns home.

How can this be? It is possible

because the return of our children is seen through eyes of faith. The father in the parable always looked and believed that his son was going to come home. This presupposes the truth that in order for the father to express this type of faith that could see the return of his child, he had to have prayed and received a promise from the Lord.

If a child, regardless of where he is and regardless of what he is doing, is a prodigal, then the prayers of his parents are crucial. His mother and father must pray daily, bombarding the throne of heaven until they receive their promise from God. Then they must go and stand watch and see, for their prodigal will come home. We parents must never, never, never give up on our children.

Two outstanding receptions are demonstrated for us in the scriptural passage about the prodigal son. The first is the father's eagerness to restore his son to fellowship. When the prodigal returned, the father ran to welcome him home and threw his arms of compassion about him. He lavishly loved him and kissed him, never rebuking him or expressing hatred or reproach. Furthermore, when the prodigal began making his confession of his unworthiness, the father cut him off by commanding a servant to clothe him with the best robe. A signet ring was put on the son's finger, indicating that the son could transact business in his father's

Your child may be cut off from your presence, but he is never cut off from the presence of the Lord.

name. This act was the visible proof of the son's restoration. Even though he had squandered his inheritance, his father was offering him another opportunity, and he proved his love by allowing him the privilege of transacting things in his name.

Another aspect of the prodigal's reception is his restoration to his position as a son. This restoration is particularly noted in the shoes which were provided for him. Sandals, which were not generally worn by servants, were brought to the prodigal. Also, his father commanded that the fattened calf should be killed to provide meat for a celebration of his son's return. The feast celebrated the father's joy at the return of his son. Although the prodigal had been cut off from the father's presence and home, he had never ceased being his father's son. He never ceased being the focus of his father's love.

If you are the parent of a prodigal, it is very important for you to follow the example of the father in this scripture. When prodigals return, they are generally filled with remorse and confession. Clothe your prodigal, parent. Clothe him with acceptance and unconditional love.

As I mentioned earlier, we parents must take comfort in the sovereignty of God. I have spoken to many young prodigals either during the time of their separation or after they have returned home, and the majority of them always tell me that the Lord hounded them most of the time when they were away. He would use incident after incident to speak to them while they were "in the pig pen." A child may be cut off from his parents' presence, but he is never cut off from the presence of the Lord. Moreover, our love for our children is as a mustard seed compared to the Lord's love for them. After all, our children are first of all His children.

Obviously, most parents have more than one child, as did the father in the parable. There was another greeting awaiting the prodigal, the one from his brother, who disapproved of the prodigal and resented his return. It appears, however, that the father apparently intervened before the elder brother said anything to the prodigal. The elder brother had been born into privilege and fellowship with the father, yet he never experienced what was available to him. Rather than showing the joyful heart of the father who welcomed home the prodigal, the elder brother showed the hardness of his heart by rejecting his wandering sibling.

When a prodigal returns home, his parents must understand that there may be those who are not as elated as they. Siblings may especially resent the fact of a prodigal being able to return into the house of their father and their mother, with whom they have stayed throughout the years. But like the father in the parable, we love all of our children. And like this father, we may be required to intervene between siblings upon the return of a prodigal child. In the Bible, the father wisely focused on what had been found rather than what had been lost when he spoke with the elder son. This must be our focus also.

IN SUMMARY

Although we may have already had our hearts broken by a prodigal child, we can take hope in the truth that a great many prodigals return home.

The first of the two reasons that children leave is the claim that "faith just didn't work" for them. Others may have become disillusioned with Christianity because their faith was not really authentic to begin with.

The second reason is that they "want more than what Christianity offers," and that is generally material possessions, popularity, or worldly lifestyle.

Waiting in faith helps us to see our prodigal children while they are yet a great while off.

We parents may have to wisely intervene in love between siblings when a prodigal child returns.

PART V
POWER OF
THE PROMISE

Chapter Fifteen

Love
Never Fails

I began the Introduction to this book by quoting from a song a mother sang to her son. She said that if she could, she would have changed the world into which she brought him: "But I would–if I could."[1] The primary purpose of this book is to try to show parents that we can change the world into which we bring our children. I have attempted to explain to you how our culture has fallen into its current state of deterioration and to emphasize the powerful influence of our culture in shaping the way we think as parents. I have gone on to relate that the foundations of our nation's values system must be changed. We must go back and lay good substructures so that the superstructures of our children's lives can withstand that which life hurls against them. And I have admonished that, most importantly, we must learn that we can no longer get by just talking the talk, and not walking the walk in our homes. If we are to succeed in changing ourselves, our children and our nation, we must learn to humbly walk in perpetual repentance.

From somewhere deep within, we should experience moral outrage as we view the condition of our society and its destructively demoralizing effect upon our children. This moral outrage may demand sacrifice from us. It may be a small sacrifice, or it may be a great sacrifice, but our generation must shoulder the responsibility of our times and make a change.

If we look at the immensity of the problem, then we may grow fainthearted, shrug and say, "There's nothing I can do." But there *is* something we can do. There is something we *must* do. We must remember the specks of sand that make up the beaches that hold back the power of the ocean and realize that we and our children are those specks of sand.

I think I have found a promise that sums up everything I have been trying to explain. It is a very powerful promise in three little words, and I found it in the Bible. Speak these three words out loud, placing the emphasis on the italicized words. These words are your promise.

Love never fails.

Love *never* fails.

Love never *fails*.

Notes

INTRODUCTION

[1]Miller Ronald L., Kenny Hirsch, and Martha V. Sharon. "If I Could," 1997.

CHAPTER 1: Revolution of Our Culture

[1]Ragni, Jerome and James Rado. "Aquarius, Let the Sunshine In," United Artists Music Co., Inc., 1970.

[2]Gottlieb, Annie. "Do You Believe in Magic?" Time, 1987. 234-35.

[3]Hays, Lee and Pete Seeger. "If I Had a Hammer," New York: Ludlow Music, Inc., 1962.

[4]Dylan, Bob. "Blowin' in the Wind," Warner Bros, Inc., 1962.

[5]Psalm 11:30

[6]II Timothy 3:1-5

CHAPTER 3: Redemption of Our Culture

[1]Matthew 5:13-16

CHAPTER 4: Observation of Tradition

[1]Deuteronomy 6:4-9

[2]Luke 24:32

[3]Deuteronomy 6:7-9

[4]Swindoll, Charles R. The Strong Family. Grand Rapids, Zondervan Publishing House, 1991. 20-21.

[5]Ibid. 21.

[6]Ibid-.

[7]Ibid. 21,-22.

[8]Strassfeld, Michael. The Jewish Holidays, New York: Harper & Row, 1985. 7.

[9]Ibid. 7.

CHAPTER 5: Objectives in Training - Spiritual Legacy

[1]Collins, Elizabeth. God Speaks Today. Unpublished manuscript, 1983. 15.

[2]Matthew 6:14, 15

CHAPTER 6: Objectives in Training - Emotional Legacy

[1]Robertson, Joel C. Help Yourself. Nashville: Thomas Nelson, 1992. 105.

[2]Ephesians 6:12

[3]Robertson, Joel C. Help Yourself. Nashville: Thomas Nelson, 1992. 105-107.

[4]Matthew 22:34-41

CHAPTER 7: Objectives in Training - Social Legacy

[1]I John 3:14

[2]I Corinthians 13:4, 5

[3]Hartley, Hermine. The Family Book of Manners Uhrichsville, Ohio: Barbour & Company, Inc.

[4]Ibid-.

CHAPTER 8: Objectives in Training - Physical Legacy

[1]Psalms 139:14

[2]Deuteronomy 6:7

[3]Bennett, William J. The Death of Outrage. New York: The Free Press, A Division of Simon & Schuster Inc.,1998. 18.

[4]Wolfenbarger, Jr., Gene. When Hollywood Says Yes, How Can America Say No? Green Forest, Arkansas: New Leaf Press, Inc., 1998. 98.

[5]Ibid. 104.

[6]Ibid. 105.

[7]Ibid.

[8]Ibid.

[9]Ibid. 101.

[10]Ibid. 107.

[11]Ibid. 106, 107.

CHAPTER 9: Objectives in Training - Moral Legacy

[1]Psalms 106: 37

[2]Psalms 106: 35-40

[3]Ezekiel 3:20, 21

[4]MacArthur, Jr., John F. The Vanishing Conscience. Dallas: Word Publishing, 1994. 182.

[5]Medved, Michael. Hollywood Vs. America. New York: Harper Collins Publishers, Inc., 1992. 33.

[6]Ibid. 186.

[7]Ibid. 243.

[8]Ibid. 244.

[9]Ibid. 244, 245.

[10]Ibid. 78.

[11]Ibid. 79.

[12]Swindoll, Charles R. The Strong Family. Grand Rapids: Zondervan Publishing House, 1991. 62.

CHAPTER 10: Realizing Our Position - Section I

[1]Malachi 4:6

[2]Matthew 18:22

[3]Collins, Elizabeth. God Speaks Today. Unpublished manuscript, 1983. 111.

[4]Swindoll, Charles R. The Strong Family. Grand Rapids: Zondervan Publishing House, 1991. 30-31.

[5]I Thessalonians 2:7

[6]I Thessalonians 2:11

[7]Ephesians 6:4

[8]Shedd, Charlie W. You Can Be a Great Parent. Waco, Texas: Word Books, 1970. 16.

Chapter 11: Realizing Our Position - Section II

[1]Genesis 18:5

[2]Judges 19:5

[3]Psalms 119:50

[4]Job 7:14

[5]Romans 15:4

[6]I Thessalonians 2:11

[7]Bennett, William J. The Death of Outrage. (New York: The Free Press, A Division of Simon & Schuster Inc., 1998. 136-137.

CHAPTER 12: Resolving Our Problem

[1]Philippians 4:13

[2]Psalms 51:2, 10, 14

[3]II Corinthians 7:10

[4]Luke 18:23

[5]Matthew 27:3, 4

[6]Psalm 51:5

[7]Psalm 51:6

[8]Romans 2:4

[9]II Chronicles 7:14

CHAPTER 13: Parenting the Potential Prodigal

[1]Carter, William Lee. The Angry Teenager. Nashville: Thomas Nelson Publishers, 1995. 35-36.

[2]Ibid. 187-188.

[3]Ibid. 192-193.

CHAPTER 14: Problems of the Prodigal

[1]Luke 15:17

[2]Luke 15:18

[3]Luke 15:19

[4]Luke 15:20

CHAPTER 15: Love Never Fails

[1]Miller, Ronald, Kenny Hirsch, and Martha V. Sharon. "If I Could." 1997.

lost generation

252

ORDER FORM

Name _____

Address _____ City _____

State _____ Zip _____ Phone _____

	Quantity	$ Total
VIDEOS: ($15.00 each)		
Laugh Out Loud - COMEDY	_____	_____
A Different Number - COMEDY	_____	_____
Three Men Who Said No to God	_____	_____
Your Encouragement - Your Responsibility	_____	
(includes Holly Ragle's story;		
Jamey's handicapped daughter)		
Birthmarks of a Believer	_____	_____
Families in the Balance	_____	_____
The High Cost of Low Living	_____	_____
A Faith Tested is a Faith Trusted	_____	_____
How to Raise Your Marriage from the Dead	_____	_____
For God So Loved (John 3:16)	_____	_____
When Daylight Dawns on Your Dirty Little Secret	_____	_____

MUSIC: ($15.00 each cassette or CD)

	Quantity	$ Total
I'm Not Alone - Jamey in solo (cassette / CD)	_____	_____
First Love - trio (cassette / CD)	_____	_____
First Love - *Songs We Remember* - hymns	_____	_____
(CD / cassette - circle one)		

CASSETTE TAPE SERIES:

	Quantity	$ Total
Good Medicine - 4-tape set ($25.00 each)	_____	_____
Survival Kit for Life -		
8 messages taped live at Liberty University		
- packaged in a nice album - ($50.00 each)	_____	_____

Shipping and handling per number of items:
1-2 = $3.00; 3-5 = $5.00; 6-10 = $7.00   S&H   _____
                    GRAND TOTAL: _____

CHARGE CARD: VISA   MASTERCARD   AMEX   DISCOVER
          Card # _____ / _____ / _____ / _____
          Expiration Date _____ / _____ Signature _____
                    Personal checks are gladly accepted

❑ Enclosed is my additional gift for Holly's House Ministry - Amount $_____
❑ Please send me information on "*Trail Mix*" - tape-of-the-month club
❑ Please send me information on becoming a *LifeBuilder* supporter of Life Building
      Ministries

Mail to: **Life Building Ministries**, PO Box 840, Burlington, KY 41005
www.jameyragle.org or info@jameyragle.org

253